GETTING BACK IN THE RACE

The Cure for Backsliding

Joel R. Beeke
Cruciform Press | Released November, 2011

To Lois Mol,
loyal and faithful friend.
"I thank my God upon every
remembrance of you." (Philippians 1:3)
– Joel R. Beeke

CruciformPress

"This book is a masterpiece, and I do not say that lightly. Since Octavius Winslow wrote his magnificent book, *Personal Declension and Revival of Religion in the Soul* in 1841, not much has seen the light of day on the vital subject of backsliding, to which every believer is prone and from which every child of God needs deliverance. This excellent work, so helpfully spiced with quotations from the Puritans, needs to be read over and over again. I heartily commend it."

Martin Holdt, Pastor, Emmanuel Baptist Church, Johannesburg, South Africa; editor *Reformation Africa South*

"Solidly written in the vein of older classics on this subject by authors like Richard Sibbes and Andrew Fulller, this new work by Dr. Beeke provides a helpful approach to what is a perennial problem for the church. For inevitably there are wounded in the spiritual war in which we are engaged, and this work outlines the best means of bringing balm and healing to their souls. Highly recommended."

Michael Haykin, author; Professor of Church History and Biblical Spirituality; Director, The Andrew Fuller Center for Baptist Studies, The Southern Baptist Theological Seminary

"*Getting Back in the Race* is a thorough treatment of the difficult subject of backsliding. It bears all the classic hallmarks of Joel Beeke's writings: it is thoroughly scriptural, warmly pastoral, saturated with the best of Puritan wisdom, and relevant for all Christians. Any of us may drop out of the race; Joel Beeke will help us prevent that happening by showing why it does happen and how it can be overcome. May this book help us to stay the course all the way to the finishing line!"

Iain D. Campbell, Minister, Point Free Church; 2012 Moderator, Free Church of Scotland General Assembly

"The strength and beauty of *Getting Back in the Race* is that Joel Beeke's characteristic clarity, biblical fidelity, and unflinching care as to detail and pastoral wisdom is obvious on every page. This book is an honest and sometimes chilling exposition of the seriousness of backsliding; at the same time, it unfailingly breathes the air of grace and hope. Timely and judicious, a book to read, re-read."

Derek W. H. Thomas, Minister of Preaching and Teaching, First Presbyterian Church, Columbia, SC; Distinguished Visiting Professor of Systematic and Historical Theology, Reformed Theological Seminary; Editorial Director, Alliance of Confessing Evangelicals

"'Don't settle for being a spiritual shrimp,' argues Dr. Beeke. The pity is that too many modern Christians are opting for shrimpishly small degrees of grace. Indwelling sin drags the careless believer down into guilty backsliding. This book is a prescription for the believer who feels his guilt. Here is medicine from the Bible ornamented with choice quotations from the great Puritans. These are healing fountains for backslidden saints."

Maurice Roberts, Minister of Greyfriars Congregation, Inverness, Scotland; former editor, *Banner of Truth* magazine

"Once again, Christian believers young and old are indebted to Joel Beeke. Dr. Beeke writes on a subject we hear much too little about, backsliding, and does so with biblical clarity, theological insight, yet always with a pastor's heart. Only too easily can even well-taught Christians find their hearts growing cold and their zeal for Christ's honor flagging. Dr. Beeke, like the spiritual physician he is, exposes to us the reasons why backsliding happens and how God in his grace maps out for us the way back to spiritual health. This is a book for all Christians, certainly not only for those who are in the sad state of backsliding. Prevention is always better than cure. Relevant biblical passages abound and choice quotes from the history of the church illuminate the text. This is a book every Christian should read and every pastor commend."

Reverend Ian Hamilton, Minister, Cambridge Presbyterian Church, Cambridge, England

CruciformPress
something new in Christian publishing

Our Books: Short. Clear. Concise. Helpful. Inspiring. Gospel-focused. *Print; ebook formats: Mobi, ePub, PDF.*

Monthly Releases: A new book the first day of every month.

Consistent Prices: Every book costs the same.

Subscription Options: Print books or ebooks delivered to you every month, at a discount. Or buy print books or ebooks individually.

Annual or Monthly Subscriptions

Print Book	$6.49 per month
Ebook	$3.99 per month

Non-Subscription Sales

1-5 Print Books	$8.45 each
6-50 Print Books	$7.45 each
More than 50 Print Books	$6.45 each
Single Ebooks (bit.ly/CPebks)	$5.45 each

Getting Back in the Race: The Cure for Backsliding

Print ISBN:	978-1-936760-35-0
ePub ISBN:	978-1-936760-36-7
Mobipocket ISBN:	978-1-936760-37-4

Table of Contents

Introduction
RUNNING WITH ENDURANCE

At the height of World War II, the enemy Axis powers controlled all of Europe from France westward, plus portions of Africa, Asia, and China. The Russian Allies were under siege in Moscow and had already lost Kiev. It seemed the unthinkable was happening: the exhausted Allies were losing their war against a merciless foe.

In October 1941 the English Prime Minister, Winston Churchill, spoke to his countrymen, and indeed to the entire free world. The substance of his message was clear: "Never, never, never give up!" Churchill called his people to persevere, and persevere they did unto victory, four long years later.

As in military conflict, so in the ongoing war that is the Christian life: perseverance like that of a marathon runner is a necessity—even, and especially, in the face of what seem to be daunting odds. Of course, in one sense this spiritual war is not to be compared to World War II, for the stakes are far higher. This is a war of which another Englishman, William Gurnall (1616–1679), said, "the cruelest [war] which ever was fought by men, will be found but sport and child's play to this. Alas, what is the killing of bodies to the destroying of souls?"[1] For this is nothing less than the warfare between Satan and the saints of God. It is a war of eternal consequence.

In this war too, we hear our Commander in Chief call us to follow him to the end and never, never, never give up. That's a tough assignment: following Christ is, in fact, more than a marathon. It's more like an "Ironman," the spiritual equivalent of swimming two and a half miles, biking 112 miles, and running 26 miles without a break. Christians — all Christians — must go the distance against great odds.

How do we do that? How do we keep up the pace? It's one thing to begin the Christian life, but quite another to persevere in it. It's one thing to repent and believe the gospel, but quite another to go on repenting and go on believing. The miracle of Pentecost in Acts 2:4 is great, but in some ways, Acts 2:42 is even greater: "And they continued steadfastly in the apostles' doctrine and fellowship and in breaking of bread, and in prayers." My father often said to me, "Remember, it's relatively easy to begin ministry in the church; the challenge is to maintain it — to persevere in zeal for it."

Haven't you, too, discovered that in some ways it can be harder to go on believing as a Christian than to become one in the first place? Haven't you, too, found it hard to persevere in faith when trouble or opposition arises, or when faced with the demands of daily life in such a world as this? Perhaps even now you are fearful. Perhaps you are afraid that you will fall into a defeatist attitude, saying, "I can never measure up to the demands of discipleship, so what's the use of trying? The poverty of my faith and my weakness in the face of temptation is terribly discouraging. How can I go on believing that 'God is light' even in the darkest night? How can I persevere in paying the high cost of faithfulness, enduring affliction and opposition and loss for the gospel's sake?"

Every Christian faces numerous discouragements in striving to follow Christ. Our knees go weak and our hands hang down when we face personal failure, when others let us down, or when providence denies our desires. Disappointment can lead to discouragement, and discouragement may end in doubt, fear, and even despair. We feel weak and tired, emotionally and spiritually, and we are tempted to throw in the towel. Why should we persist in confessing a faith that is despised and hated in the world? It all seems pointless and hopeless. We say with Asaph, "Verily I have cleansed my heart in vain" (Psalm 73:13).

But we must press on, firm in the confidence that we run alongside other believers, that we run a well-trodden course, and that we run with God's inexhaustible assistance and support. J. C. Ryle (1816–1900) said, "We have a race to run," and went on to explain that every true Christian must endure great opposition:

> Without there will be fightings, within there will be fears; there will be snares to be avoided, and

temptations to be resisted; there will be your own treacherous hearts, often cold and dead and dry and dull; there will be friends who will give you unscriptural advice, and relations who will even war against your soul; in short, there will be stumbling-blocks on every side, there will be occasion for all your diligence and watchfulness and godly jealousy and prayer, you will soon find that to be a real Christian is no light matter.[2]

But the Lord does not call us to go where he has not gone before. We are called to endure what Christ endured before us, to follow the course he has already taken. Hebrews 12:1–2 says,

> Let us lay aside every weight, and the sin which doth so easily beset us, and let us run with patience the race that is set before us, looking unto Jesus the author and finisher of our faith; who for the joy that was set before him endured the cross, despising the shame, and is set down at the right hand of the throne of God.

There's the key: "looking unto Jesus." The more we fix our eyes on the glory of the one who died and rose and now sits at God's right hand, the more we will press on to meet him. John Bunyan (1628–1688), himself no stranger to hardship, said, "When men do come to see the things of another world, what a God, what a Christ, what a heaven, and what an eternal glory there is to be enjoyed; also, when they see that it is possible for them to have a share in it, I tell you it will make them run through thick and thin to enjoy it."[3]

But when we lose sight of Christ because of our sin, or Satan's lies, we grow tired and weak. We begin to lose our bearings, drift out of the way, or else give up too soon. Let's take a lesson from American swimmer Florence Chadwick (1918–1995). While I am not the first to tell her story, it is well worth recounting here. In her prime, she swam the English Channel in record time. But when she attempted to swim the 26 miles from Catalina Island to the coast of California, a thick fog set in after fifteen hours in the water. She could no longer see her goal, so she grew discouraged. Finally, an hour later, she asked to be pulled out by the people in boats accompanying her. Imagine her dismay when she discovered that she was only one mile from her goal! Two months later she tried again, and the same fog set in. But this time she fixed in her mind an image of the shore ahead of her, and pressed on to reach her goal.

When sin or unbelief or false teaching make it hard to see Jesus, Christians grow discouraged, become weak in faith, and may begin to turn away from the Lord. Like a swimmer in the fog, our own sins constantly block our view of the glorious goal, so we are tempted to abandon the pursuit entirely. This turning away from Christ is often called backsliding: a drawing back from God, from our profession of faith, and from our commitment to follow Christ. To backslide is to relapse into unbelief, sin, and spiritual numbness. Backsliding is an act of disloyalty and a form of rebellion. It can happen to an individual, a family, a church, even a whole denomination. Backsliding can leave people in a weakened spiritual condition for years before they recover. It can even lead to final apostasy, giving up and walking away from the Lord forever.

The purpose of this book is to awaken Christians to the reality of backsliding, to help us recognize it when it starts, to show where it may lead, and to empower believers—those who are in the grip of backsliding, or those in a position to help the afflicted—to get back into the race by the grace of God. We will first analyze the spiritual disease of backsliding, then proceed to the divine cure.[4]

This book will also introduce you to the vast body of helpful literature on backsliding and spiritual experience in general. Christian writers of the seventeenth, eighteenth, and nineteenth centuries gave considerable attention to the problem of backsliding. Many of their books continue to be printed today. Strangely, treatment of this topic has become quite rare among recent authors. Therefore, I hope to introduce you to some of the old writers of the Reformed and Puritan traditions who handle spiritual experience with biblical wisdom. Follow the footnotes of this book like bridges to other valuable books.

I encourage you to read this book with prayer. Pray that the Holy Spirit would illuminate your mind to see the truth, and bring your heart captive to love for the truth. Pray also for your church and other Christians, that God would heal all our backsliding (Hosea 14:4).

I believe in both the preservation of the saints by God

and the perseverance of the saints before God. True, our perseverance is a fruit of God's preservation, but that perseverance is still ours, a fight we must fight and a race we must run. It doesn't happen objectively outside of us; it happens subjectively, by grace, within us and through us. Trusting in God, looking to Christ, and relying on the help of the Holy Spirit in using the spiritual disciplines, we must run the race and we must finish the course. We are no mere spectators, nor can we remain on the sidelines. Every Christian is a runner.

We must continue on patiently, ploddingly, believing in the Lord—not only in times of prosperity, but also in times of adversity. May God use this book to strengthen you and keep you running in the race until you reach the goal, obtain the prize, and receive your crown from the hand of Christ in glory!

One
RUNNERS STUMBLING

Discerning Backsliding

Picture a runner in a long-distance, cross-country race. Off the mark, things look great. He sets a strong pace, feels good, and can see victory ahead. But as the race progresses he grows over-confident and careless. He stops paying attention to the terrain. Instead he dreams about the shouts of admiration when he crosses the finish line in record time. After running strongly for a while, he fails to see a dip in the path and falls. In an instant he finds himself on the ground, knees bloodied and head throbbing, his face in the dirt. He feels confused, discouraged, and embarrassed. So he lies there, unsure whether to give up or keep going.

This is a difficult situation, and a moment of crisis. The runner has reason to feel ashamed of himself. *But he need not give up*. He can finish the race, and finish it well. So can you, if you are a backslidden Christian who has fallen into sin through your own weakness and carelessness. By the grace of God, I will do all I can in the following pages to show you how to position yourself to receive from God the understanding, the humility, and the courage to get back in the race. And if you are currently running strong in the Lord, I trust this book can serve you in two ways: to equip you to help others get up and keep going, and to prepare yourself (God forbid) for the possibility of your own backsliding in the future.

What Is Backsliding?

Backsliding is a season of increasing sin and decreasing obedience in those who profess to be Christians. *Not every sin is backsliding.* Christians must sadly expect their lives to consist of a continual cycle of sinning and repenting of sin by faith in Christ crucified (1 John 1:9–2:2). In backsliding, however, this cycle of repentance is broken and spiritual ground is lost. Wilhelmus à Brakel (1635–1711) described backsliding as "spiritual winter" in one's life, "the very opposite of growth."[5] Andrew Fuller (1754–1815) defined backsliding among professing Christians as "their having sinned, and not repented of their deeds."[6] Edward Reynolds (1599–1676) called it "a repenting of repentance."[7] The longer one persists in backsliding, the less right one has to claim to be a true Christian (1 John 2:3–4), for repentance is of the essence of true Christianity (Acts 2:38, 20:21; 26:18, 20).

All throughout the Bible, we are warned about backsliding.[8] The Lord used His prophets Hosea and Jeremiah more than any others to admonish Israel and the church of all ages of this evil.[9] The prophetic rebuke of backsliding revealed Israel's turning away from the Lord as nothing less than adultery against her divine husband:

God's wife engaged in spiritual prostitution with rival lovers (Jeremiah 3, Hosea 4).

Backsliding from Christ is thus a serious matter. It dishonors God, disregards Christ as Savior, grieves the Spirit, tramples God's law underfoot, and abuses the gospel. In other words, to backslide means to depart from the Word and the ways of the Lord. Nevertheless, in every age it has been, and remains, a sin as common as it is terrible.

Bent to Backsliding

Although the apostle James did not use the word "backslide," he addressed the same adulterous love of the world among the churches (James 4:1–10). Only a couple of decades after Christ ascended into heaven and poured out the Holy Spirit, churches and Christians were backsliding! And this tendency was nothing new. In words recorded some 700 years earlier, we hear the Lord lamenting, "my people are bent to backsliding from me" (Hosea 11:7). The word "people" here refers to God's people in general—what we would call today the visible church. It thus includes those who profess faith but have no true heart for the Lord. Of these, Jeremiah Burroughs (c. 1600–1646) wrote, "There is a principle of apostasy in them. . . . God's ways have been unsuitable to them, and therefore they have found them hard and tedious."[10]

Notice how Hosea 11:7 says "bent," not just "bendable." Ebenezer Erskine (1680–1754) wrote, "There is not only an easiness and ductility [flexibility] in the heart of man to sin, but a strong propensity and inclination."[11] Scripture and history alike bear it out: the church has a strong inclination to backslide. Like a man standing on an icy hill by a sharp drop, one misstep can begin a slide towards destruction.

But backsliding is certainly not limited to unbelievers, to hypocrites in the church, or to the church in general (a mixture of Christians and those who profess faith but do not possess it). The same tendency exists for those who are God's true runners in the race. These can backslide too, missing out on heavenly rewards they might have otherwise obtained.

Consider this analogy of how easily we can slip into backsliding. Going into the 10,000 meter event in the 2010 Olympics, Sven Kramer of the Netherlands was positioned well to win his second speed skating gold medal. In fact, when the race came, he completed the course in record time. Tragically, however, he had disqualified himself by skating in the wrong lane for part of the race, following the mistaken advice of his coach. Any athlete can tell you that your performance means nothing unless you follow the rules. That's why Paul wrote in 2 Timothy 2:5 that if a man competes in the games, he will not receive the victor's crown unless he competes according to the rules. If we are "skating in the wrong lane," that is, backsliding in our obedience to God's commands, it does not matter how well we think we are doing or how much admiration others may have for us. We must run in God's ways — according to his will, not our own.

As we run our daily race, sinfully crossing over the lines God has set for us can happen almost effortlessly. William S. Plumer (1802–1880) said,

It is easy for us to backslide from God. We go astray from the womb, speaking lies. It is as natural for us to do wrong as for the sparks to ascend. In our voyage heavenward, wind and tide are against us. If we do nothing to overcome their action, they will carry us away. We can go to hell without intending to do so, without putting forth any efforts to that effect. But to go to heaven requires prayer, self-denial, vigilance, violence, running, wrestling, fighting.[12]

Plumer is right: this Christian life is a war, not against men, but against ourselves, the system of the world, and the devil.

If backsliding occurred even once in our lives as Christians, it would be unspeakably grievous and heinous. God has loved us with an everlasting love, forgiven all our sins, embraced us as his children, and blessed us with every spiritual blessing. To backslide even once merely in thought would be more than sufficient reason, in human reckoning, for God to withdraw his love from us. But the real state of things is worse—much worse. Hosea says we are bent—inclined, directed, habituated—to backsliding, despite the immeasurable depth of God's love. If left to ourselves, we will continually backslide from the Lord. Is this not as true of you as it is of me?

Just as sin is not made less awful or less offensive to God by its prevalence, so our shared bent to backsliding does not render that bent a trivial matter. God surely *does* promise that wherever he begins the good work of salvation, he will bring it to completion (Philippians 1:6).

But this does not allow us to be passive and apathetic in the face of our backsliding tendencies. Thomas Vincent (1634–1678) warned that God preserves his people through their motives and their efforts to use the means of grace God provides. We must avail ourselves of the grace that God grants us.

Furthermore, God's preservation does not guarantee that we will avoid sad falls. Vincent warned his hearers: "Though God will not allow you totally to fall from grace if the good work is in truth begun in you, yet, without great heed, you may fall into great decay of grace; your graces may languish and so be ready to die (Revelation 3:2)."[13] What might that look like practically? Vincent continued, "You may fall foully into sin" so that you shame the name of Christ, wound your conscience, grieve the Spirit, hurt the church, interrupt your fellowship with God, lose your assurance of salvation, and fall under God's discipline.[14] Frightful, yes, but all of it true.

Taking Stock

Perhaps there was a time in your life when you would not have believed these words of Hosea 11:7—a time when, in the flush of first love, prayer was your daily breath and the Word of God your daily food. At that time, the word "backsliding" was foreign to your vocabulary. Sin was sin, grace was grace, God was God, and Christ was Christ. You would have waded through hell itself to get to Jesus Christ.[15] The Lord could say of you, "I remember thee, the kindness of thy youth, the love of thine espousals, when thou wentest after me in the wilderness, in a land that was not sown" (Jeremiah 2:2). Like Joseph you dreaded the thought of sinning against God (Genesis 39:9).

But how is your spiritual life now? Do you have a different understanding? Perhaps you must say, "It is all true; I am prone to backslide. I am inclined to wander from the narrow path, to go astray like a lost sheep, to return to a life I thought I'd left behind forever. 'For I know that in me (that is, in my flesh) dwelleth no good thing' (Romans 7:18). My only hope remains Psalm 40:2, for '*He* brought me up also out of an horrible pit, out of the miry clay, and set my feet upon a rock, and established my goings.'"

How do God's people fall into the ever-deepening rut and horrible pit of backsliding? How does the sin of backsliding extend its deadly influence through their entire spiritual and natural lives? What marks should I look for in myself to know if I am backsliding? These are all crucial questions.

Signs of Sliding into a Spiritual Rut

God's people let themselves drift. We fall into backsliding gradually, a process unfolding over time. This is no surprise, for apart from the grace of God we remain children of Adam our entire lives. We can never shake off our old nature completely; it clings to us with the tendrils of countless sinful tendencies.

The life of God's child is illustrated in a frequent scene in rural Michigan during the winter weeks of heavy snow.

The lanes and smaller roads, many of them unpaved, become muddy and nearly impassable. Looking down these after a snow, at first only one set of tracks appears. As each subsequent vehicle follows the same tracks, the ruts grow increasingly deeper, until someone finally becomes stuck and can go no further.

Similarly, God's children are prone to follow the tracks of their muddy human nature, following those tracks wherever they lead. The further they go, the deeper they sink into the ruts, step by step, one thing leading to another, until they get stuck. What are these ruts believers are so inclined to fall into? I can enumerate at least these six:

1. Coldness in prayer
2. Indifference under the Word
3. Growing inner corruptions
4. The love of the world
5. Declining love for believers
6. Man-centered hopes

I will present much of what follows in the second person, as if I am speaking directly to a backslidden saint. I do this not to accuse or condemn you, the reader—the main point of this book is that grace and healing through Christ is freely available!—but to give you opportunity to more easily see yourself in whatever sections may apply. Few things are more important in the Christian life than to recognize when backsliding has set in.

Coldness in prayer. Formerly, it was a delight to your soul to anticipate going to pray. You longed to be alone with the Lord, to speak with him, and to pour out your heart before him with all your needs, confessions, and vows. You spread out every matter before the Lord as if he knew nothing about it, yet with a deep consciousness that he always knows your circumstances and your needs better than you do.

Gradually, however, your zeal in prayer begins to fade away. Before you realize it, your prayers become more a matter of words than heart. Alexander Ross says, "A man may pray with his lips and yet not pray with an intense desire of the soul."[16] Form and coldness increasingly replace love and urgency. The Lord warned of this danger in Isaiah 29:13, saying "this people draw near me with their mouth, and with their lips do honour me, but have removed their heart far from me."

Before long, morning prayer is all but given up; you no longer feel it is critical to call on God to begin your day rightly. Prayer at bedtime shortens, and wandering thoughts during prayer multiply. Prayer throughout the day largely vanishes. James 4:2 begins to describe you: "ye have not, because ye ask not." God formed you to declare his praise, but now he says to you, "thou hast not called upon me, O Jacob; but thou hast been weary of me, O Israel" (Isaiah 43:22). Fuller warned, "If religious duties are attended to rather from custom or conscience than love, we must either never have known what true religion is, or in a great degree have lost the spirit of it."[17]

Formality and deadness conquer power and access. Omitting prayer may seem more reverent than actually praying. Your head is still bowed, and words are still uttered, but where is the love, urgency, necessity, and sense of dependency? Where are the heartfelt petitions for husband, wife, children, friends, colleagues, church, and nation? If the Lord gives us honesty and spiritual sight, we will see that what we have is nothing but prayerless praying, our former liberty in prayer having departed from us.

Prayerlessness arises from unbelief. The visible beauty of the world seems more important to us than anything else while the invisible, heavenly beauty of God seems less real. We lose sight of our Husband's glory and our hearts go out after cheap substitutes, false gods of our own choosing who promise much but deliver nothing. True prayer goes to the Lord as a thirsty man goes to a clear, cool river in order to drink; unbelief abandons the fountain of living water for broken cisterns that hold no water (Jeremiah 2:13).

Indifference under the Word. As you draw back from your Lord you find your affections toward God cooling. This especially shows itself in indifference towards God's Word, which can eventually lead you to lose all concern for truth. Losing your appetite for God's living and life-giving Word reveals a lack of spiritual health and forecasts further decline, for the Bible says, "As newborn babes, desire the sincere milk of the word, that ye may grow thereby" (1 Peter 2:2). It is not enough to attend preaching; one must *desire* the Word.

You do not neglect church attendance, but neither do you cherish it; the heart is not in it as before. The public means of grace substitute for a close and secret walk with God. Physically, you enter the sanctuary, but spiritually, the soul takes up its abode only in the outer courts of the temple; you can no longer bring your soul beyond the vestibule. No wonder that the minister's preaching does not seem to be so heart-searching as before; no wonder that worship services becomes more of a burden than a delight.

Backsliding may not immediately produce scandalous sins; it may begin with a cold heart. John Angell James (1785–1859) wrote, "There is no immorality; no open sin; but an utter decay of religious affections. The whole amount of piety that is left is cold, heartless, dead formality."[18] The trouble starts so quietly with the affections alone: that subtlety is its chief danger. John Newton (1725–1807) said, "Christians are often not aware how soon they may decline in their religious affections."[19]

Perhaps you still read the Bible dutifully and even regularly, but where is the spiritual relish with which you read the Word in former times? It seems but a memory that once you could say, "How sweet are thy words unto my taste! yea, sweeter than honey to my mouth!" (Psalm 119:103). Where is the former burning desire to be alone with the Word of God, even if it did nothing but convict you of sin? Where are all the holy precepts, precious promises, pointed rebukes, and instructive lessons that once abounded on its sacred pages? A dry heart finds the Bible dry as well. Your tears are too few to water the spiritual seeds in your soul. In desperation, you resort to texts that moved you before, yet to no avail. You fail to revive old manna, long since spoiled (Exodus 16:19–20).

It may even be that, like King Asa, your good begin-

nings have been marred by trusting in man instead of
the Lord, and now you are angry at the very men who
faithfully preach God's Word to you (2 Chronicles 16:10).
God's hand may be upon your conscience for some sin,
but you refuse to confess it and forsake it, so the Word
shines upon you like the hot sun in a summer drought
(Psalm 32:3–4). Beware lest you become like "children
that will not hear the law of the LORD," as described in
Isaiah 30:9–10, "Which say to the seers, See not; and to the
prophets, Prophesy not unto us right things, speak unto
us smooth things, prophesy deceits." Is it possible that the
very reason you see the preacher as your enemy is because
he tells you the truth (Galatians 4:16)?

Dryness under the Word also implies backsliding
from him who is the living and eternal Word. The center
and heart of all the means of grace, Jesus Christ, seems to
depart. He was once the substance of your life, the source
of your sanctification, and the mark towards which you
always pressed, but now he silently withdraws himself.
You no longer carry your guilt to his blood for covering
and cleansing. Instead of blaming yourself, you more
often blame the Lord, finding fault with his ministers, the
officers of the church, and your fellow church members.
Talking about religion and church affairs becomes a substitute for having Christ in the heart.

Soon, indifference produces its close companion
on the road of backsliding: ignorance. "My people are
destroyed for lack of knowledge" (Hosea 4:6). Jeremiah
lamented with tears that the Lord said of Israel, "they
know not me," and "they refuse to know me" (Jeremiah

9:3, 6). You fill your mind with the things of the world and the cares of this life while neglecting the truths of God.

As backsliding sets in among a people collectively, they willfully despise the church's confessed teachings, which results in the loss of confessional truth. The church, created by God to be the pillar of the truth (1 Timothy 3:15), descends into ignorance, confusion, vain disputations, and false teaching.

Growing inner corruptions. The secret sins of the heart begin to multiply as you neglect to put them to death. Your earnest prayer is no longer, "Search me, O God, and know my heart: try me, and know my thoughts: And see if there be any wicked way in me, and lead me in the way everlasting" (Psalm 139:23–24). Instead you cover the evidence of your sin, hiding from God and blaming others, as Adam did: "The woman whom thou gavest to be with me, she gave me of the tree" (Genesis 3:12). You once said only "I did eat," but now it becomes anyone's fault but your own—even the Lord's fault. You may not dare to say this with your mouth, but it is revealed in the practice of your life. You once lived submissive to God's sovereignty when there was any conflict between self and God: "Everything the Lord does is right and everything I do contrary to his will is wrong." But now you bend toward self and away from the Lord.

Such excuses encourage hypocrisy. Gradually, you become more interested in merely learning the language of God's people rather than experiencing for yourself the underlying realities. When you do talk of the Lord and his ways, self begins to creep in more and more, at first half-ashamed, but then losing any shame whatsoever. You may say the right things, but only to win the admiration of others. Deep in your heart, self-exaltation becomes your motivation. Spiritual pride replaces lowliness of mind.

A *double life* begins to emerge of which you may be only half-conscious. You fail to heed Christ's word to "cleanse first that which is within the cup and platter, that the outside of them may be clean also," and instead become more like whitewashed tombs, beautiful on the outside but inwardly full of uncleanness (Matthew 23:26–27). Zeal for God's cause and honor burns low, while what man thinks of you glows white-hot. You begin to try convincing others that you are living *for* God rather than trying to live *with* God.

A double life, in turn, leads to the multiplication of *secret sins*. Sins you thought long gone in grace are resurrected with even more power than before. And what is worse, you hardly tremble before sin's power. You may not run after sin as you did before regeneration, but now sin runs after you. And as your resistance against sin grows weaker, you welcome its approach. Offending God does not remain the overriding burden of sin; instead, the punishment of sin, or perhaps its offense to men, becomes your primary motive for resisting temptation. You may still confess sin as sin and make vows to change, but you do both acts as an empty show of piety. Your confession comes without repentance, and you do not follow your vows with change. You speak against sin but accommodate it in practice and, on occasion, even fuel sin, in spite of your conscience (Romans 13:14).

It may be that you comfort yourself with your outward morality and form of religion, claiming that you are "not as other men are" (Luke 18:11). But God sees the heart. His warning pierces deeper than behavior: "The backslider *in heart* shall be filled with his own ways" (Proverbs 14:14, emphasis added). We reap what we sow in this life. The backslider shall "be filled with sin, either in this world or the next, when he feels its painful consequences, and finds that God has marked all his steps, and will not acquit him from any of his iniquities [absent his repentance]."[20]

The danger is that your *self-examination* becomes less frequent, less thorough, and less prayerful. Consequently, hand-in-hand with an evaporating spiritual life, the Pharisee who is within us all comes to the forefront. Gradually, you become an inflated ("puffed up") saint with a much smaller Savior whose work, in your eyes, steadily diminishes in importance.

Presumption follows hard on the heels of decreasing self-examination. In spite of God's silence and your own failure to withstand trials, temptations, and weaknesses in your own strength, you continue to presume that all is well. Even the chastising and warning hand of God's providence passes by unheeded (Micah 6:9, Luke 13:1–5).

The love of the world. One sign of backsliding, and often the first sign others can notice, is an increase in worldliness. In everyday life, in conversation, and even in dress and fashion, the spirit of the world begins to take hold of you. The distinction between godliness and worldliness becomes increasingly difficult for you to discern, and the tendency to accommodate the ways of the world seems ever greater, never less. Instead of being a chaste spouse devoted to your Lord, you begin to flirt with the world. James warns, "Ye adulterers and adulteresses, know ye not that the friendship of the world is enmity with God? Whosoever therefore will be a friend of the world is the enemy of God" (James 4:4).

Instead of walking toward godliness and away from worldliness, you and the world begin to have more and more in common. Your motivations and inclinations begin to shift. At one time your possessions, entertainments, pursuits, and companions found their purpose and focus in Christ's kingdom, but increasingly you become allied with the world. As this happens, the world increasingly fills your days and subverts your heart. John Owen (1616–1683) said, "When the world fills our thoughts, it will entangle our affections."[21] The world consumes your heart, contrary to the stern commands and warnings of 1 John 2:15–16:

> Love not the world, neither the things that are in the world. If any man love the world, the love of the Father is not in him. For all that is in the world, the lust of the flesh, and the lust of the eyes, and the pride of life, is not of the Father, but is of the world.

Is this not what Hosea warned against when the Spirit directed him to write: "Ephraim, he hath mixed himself among the people" (Hosea 7:8)? Burroughs said, "It is a very dangerous thing to be mixed with a wicked society."[22]

Lot chose to dwell in the plains of Sodom and

Gomorrah because, as a well-watered land, it looked beautiful: "even as the garden of the LORD, like the land of Egypt" (Genesis 13:10). It was not long before he "pitched his tent towards Sodom" (verse 12). In the end, he found himself moving into that wicked city—not with his heart only, but now putting his feet into a place where he had no business being. This is not a comment about cities but about how backsliding can progress in the lives of God's people. Like Lot, you may be vexed by the world (2 Peter 2:7) but still drawn to its vanities and ideas.

Worldliness grasps God's good creations and uses them in an idolatrous or perverse manner. God's gifts become masters instead of servants:

- Money becomes your love rather than your servant in your love for Christ.
- Politics becomes your basis for hope (or despair) when you should work for justice, hoping in Christ's appearing rather than in the results of the next election.
- Music and the arts capture your mind with sensual stimulation, steal your time with worthless entertainment, or corrupt your heart with wicked content instead of serving as creative media for God's glory.
- Friends and relationships become your heaven rather than helping you along to heaven.
- Clothing ceases to serve as modest covering, protection, and adornment of your body and instead consumes your money in a bid to impress your neighbors, display your sophistication, gain attention, or express your sensuality.

Backsliding can progress so far that even the world will begin noticing your worldliness, perhaps with expressions of approval that you are not so "overly religious" anymore. Sometimes, even worldly people can be surprised at what a backsliding child of God will now do or allow.

Declining love for believers. Backsliding can advance so far that *brotherly love*, one of the most basic marks of saving grace (1 John 3:14), seems to all but disappear within you. You disagree over nominal matters with fellow believers, unwilling to set down your preferences for their sakes, and those disagreements grow into large fights. James 4:1 says, "From whence come wars and fightings among you? come they not hence, even of your lusts that war in your members?" Worldliness in church members foments wars within the church. Plumer said, "As piety thus dies in the soul, charity diminishes, and censoriousness takes its place."[23]

Your own self-promotion and self-protection can smother any thought of self-sacrifice or service to others. As this takes place collectively, God's people become strangers to one another instead of fellow pilgrims. Conflicts, troubles, disputes, and selfishness multiply. Ebenezer Erskine said, "Backsliders are commonly backbiters."[24] Of course, you convince yourself that the conflict is over truth, or some matter of consequence, but deep in your conscience you know it is really only a thinly disguised personality conflict or "turf war." Otherwise, how did you get along so well before? Instead of covering one another's faults, you now gladly take opportunities to talk against one another and defend yourselves.

People of God, can't we all say with shame that we run more *against* one another than *with* one another, as John ran with Peter? Isn't there more suspecting, mistrusting, and despising of others than love? Who among us knows how to forgive, to forbear, to suffer long, and even to suffer wrong at the hands of our brethren? Christ declared that "to whom little is forgiven, the same loveth little" (Luke 7:47). Do we so undervalue the worth of our own salvation (2 Peter 1:9)?

Man-centered hopes. Into the vacuum created by God's departing glory rushes man's love for strife and vainglory (Philippians 2:3a). Satan moves from questioning, "hath God said?" to asserting, "ye shall be as gods" (Genesis 3:1, 5). People become the center of the church, so people become the subject of all talk. People are either idolized or criticized, and God and his Word are set aside. Conversation increasingly centers on preachers and leaders, and you set yourselves up as judges of one another. One minister is good; another, fair; a third, no good at all. "You have an over-critical spirit respecting preaching."[25] You measure man by man instead of by God's Word. Thus you fall under the censure of Paul in 1 Corinthians 3:3–4, "For ye are yet carnal: for whereas there is among you envying, and strife, and divisions, are ye not carnal, and walk as men? For while one saith, I am of Paul; and another, I am of Apollos; are ye not carnal?"

You find yourself not only comparing preachers to one another, but also comparing yourself to other believers. You trust the opinion of other believers on matters of doctrine and even the state of your own soul, not consulting God in his Word or through prayer. This is no new temptation, for God warned against this kind of man-centeredness throughout the prophets. Consider Jeremiah 17:5–6:

> Thus saith the LORD; Cursed be the man that trusteth in man, and maketh flesh his arm, and whose heart departeth from the LORD. For he shall be like the heath in the desert, and shall not see when good cometh; but shall inhabit the parched places in the wilderness, in a salt land and not inhabited.

Man-centeredness is an awful curse on the church and a dreadful blasphemy of God's name, the fruit of spiritual deadness. You can have no personal blessing unless the Lord breaks it down!

Backsliding produces false assurance and feeble hope. Attaching God's name to man's activities may make you feel assured of his blessing, but this is to live in a fool's paradise of self-deception. If your hope is that feeble, you have probably aimed too low, having put your trust in men—yourself or others—rather than in God. God's people have sought false hope before, and God has frustrated those efforts, as Isaiah 31:1, 3 describes:

> Woe to them that go down to Egypt for help; and stay on horses, and trust in chariots, because they are many; and in horsemen, because they are very strong; but they look not unto the Holy One of Israel, neither seek the LORD! . . . Now the Egyptians

are men, and not God; and their horses flesh, and not spirit. When the LORD shall stretch out his hand, both he that helpeth shall fall, and he that is holpen [helped] shall fall down, and they all shall fail together.

Oh, for Christians who reject man-centered hope and live with a holy expectation in God and a proper sense of their own unworthiness! Holy expectation is built on the Word and worked by the Spirit. It looks beyond self and man. It sees that although our sins pile up to heaven, Christ's substitutionary righteousness ascends still higher, to the very throne of God, with his Father's stamp of approval. "Let Israel hope in the LORD: for with the LORD there is mercy, and with him is plenteous redemption. And he shall redeem Israel from all his iniquities" (Psalm 130:6–7).

On that basis, holy expectation intercedes at the throne of grace, pleading that the great triune God of heaven and earth would pour out his blessings. Holy expectation cannot coexist with worldliness, unbelief, indifference, and ignorance. It abhors backsliding and seeks the honor of God, the conversion of sinners, and the welfare of the church.

The church's only hope—our only hope—is in God, for God alone can reverse the damage done by backsliding. Only God can revive the backsliding of a single believer or an entire church. Pray that God would remember us in Christ Jesus, send forth his indispensable Spirit, and revive both our churches and us. May sons and daughters again be born in Zion, and may the old nature be crucified, the world despised, Satan resisted, and interceders at the throne of grace multiplied. May God himself receive his rightful place among us by divine conquest, so that Christ will become all in all for us (Colossians 3:11) and we might become increasingly conformed to his image as the firstborn among many brethren (Romans 8:29).

The Bitter Results of Backsliding

We have established that we are "bent to backsliding," and we have discussed signs of backsliding. But what are the results of such sinfulness? Where will it lead? Allow me to mention just four bitter fruits.

Injury to God's holy and worthy name. When David committed adultery and murder, and then covered it up, God rebuked him, saying, "Wherefore hast thou despised the commandment of the LORD, to do evil in his sight? . . . thou hast despised me. . . . because by this deed thou hast given great occasion to the enemies of the LORD to blaspheme" (2 Samuel 12:9, 10, 14). How men will mock at Christ when they hear that those bearing his name acted shamefully!

The worst thing about backsliding is that it casts discredit on the name of the God who has given us so much grace. How it should wound God's people daily: "I am a backslider against him who gave himself up to death, who for six long, torturous hours hung upon a cross while mockers stood before him, saying, 'Come down if thou be the Christ.'" The life of a backslider is an insult to Christ's love displayed for us at the cross.

Our own suffering. Backsliding causes a believer inwardly to experience more deadness than life, more rebellion than reconciliation, and more false peace than real peace.

There are times when conscience awakens and begins to roar (Psalm 32:3–4; 38:3–4), for God disciplines his children, but we should not underestimate his power to afflict us for our own good (Hebrews 12:4–11). That is, sometimes God's discipline appears more harsh than kind. Brakel wrote,

> Are you brazen toward the Lord? . . . Consider that God will not put up with your sulking. "He is wise in heart, and mighty in strength: who hath hardened himself against him, and hath prospered?" (Job 9:4). God may come and make life so bitter for you, that for the remainder of your life you will lament that you have been so rancorous toward the Lord. Therefore, take care that you regress no further.[26]

If unchecked, backsliding leads to apostasy and damnation. For all sin tends to hell, and therefore must be dealt with severely. Our Lord said in Matthew 5:30, "And if thy right hand offend thee, cut it off, and cast it from thee: for it is profitable for thee that one of thy members should perish, and not that thy whole body should be cast into hell." John Angell James expanded on this ethic with this counsel: "Do not attempt while the sinful practice is continued, to gain any comfort of mind by the supposition that you are a true Christian still, and shall one day be restored to God by penitence and faith."[27] Fuller similarly warned, "So long as sin remains upon the conscience unlamented, we are in danger of eternal damnation."[28]

This is not to deny the perseverance of the elect, for election produces holiness (Ephesians 1:4). The security of the elect must never be separated from their perseverance in repentance as well as in faith. "Nevertheless the foundation of God standeth sure, having this seal, The Lord knoweth them that are his. And, let every one that nameth the name of Christ depart from iniquity" (2 Timothy 2:19). If you want to find peace in the doctrine of election, you must repent and pursue holiness, and show yourself elect. As long as you rest in sin, you are on a trajectory towards hell.

The sin and apostasy of our children. It is not uncommon for children to follow their parents in sin "unto the third and fourth generation" (Exodus 20:5). It sometimes is even the case that when a believer backslides by clinging to a cherished sin for a time, his children grasp hold of his favorite sin or idol and carry it all the way to hell. Lot was vexed by the wickedness of Sodom (2 Peter 2:7), but his attachment to that unholy city made him lose his wife and his daughters to worldliness and wantonness (Genesis 19). David repented of his sins, but his adultery and murder were followed by his son Amnon raping his half-sister Tamar; another son, Absalom, became a deceiver, usurper, and traitor to David's own throne. Shall we pray for our children's salvation with our mouths but point them to damnation with our actions?

The decay of the church. Bad company corrupts

good morals (1 Corinthians 15:33). One person within the church whose heart is turning away from the Lord is like "a root bearing gall and wormwood" (Deuteronomy 29:18, Hebrews 12:15). Using a similar metaphor, Paul warned that there comes a time when the church must remove such influences from the body to prevent further corruption (see 1 Corinthians 5:6b–7).

Even a godly man like Barnabas could be led astray into hypocrisy if Peter stumbled (Galatians 2:13). Do you want to be the cause of others stumbling? One slow-moving truck can back up traffic; one accident on the highway can create a traffic jam stretching for miles. You are not an island, standing alone. Your progress towards Christ or backsliding from him affects many others.

Conclusion

Do you know what the greatest evil of such backsliding is? *We do not feel any guilt for it.* We complain about spiritual dryness, the darkness of the times, the sad condition of the church and of God's people, but what does the Lord say of such complaints? They are nothing more than empty words in his ears if we do not repent of our role in causing the deadness and darkness: "I hearkened and heard, but they spake not aright: no man repented him of his wickedness, saying, What have I done? Everyone turned to his course, as the horse rusheth into the battle" (Jeremiah 8:6). Where are the Jeremiahs today who can say with heart and soul, "For the hurt of the daughter of my people am I hurt; I am black; astonishment hath taken hold on me" (Jeremiah 8:21)?

Can you say as God's child that your backsliding has cut bitter furrows in your life—furrows of pain and sorrow in the depths of your soul? Does it cut your soul into a thousand pieces before the Lord? Does it make you to cry out in spiritual anguish, "O Lord, what a fool, what a backsliding wretch I am! If only I could tear out my heart and cast it far from me! I abhor myself and repent in dust and ashes!" Join with Jeremiah in saying, "Oh that my head were waters, and mine eyes a fountain of tears, that I might weep day and night for the slain of the daughter of my people!" (Jeremiah 9:1). Only when godly sorrow brings you to such a point can you take the first step toward the healing of your backsliding.

Two
RUNNERS RETURNING

The Physician of Grace (Hosea 14:1-3)

A serious runner who suffers even a fairly minor injury, if he intends to remain a competitor, will seek out the best physician available to him. He knows that without proper medical attention his days as a strong contender could quickly limp to a halt. Most of us, however, are not that wise or vigilant. We tend to be ambivalent about doctors and health regimens, even when we secretly suspect something is wrong. Indeed, it is not unusual for someone with a confirmed condition, something chronic and potentially serious, to neglect the doctor's orders and resist the regular visits and treatments required to stave off further decline. When it comes to our physical health, we often act as though our problems are not all that bad — even while we fear they are very bad indeed.

It is the same with our spiritual condition. When there is a lack of health in the soul, few among us will consistently face the truth and respond accordingly. Even when, by the wisdom of God's Word, we come to know the precise prescription for our healing, as well as the inevitable decline that will result from inaction, we prefer the ease of idleness.

The fact is that when it comes to diseases of the soul, we desperately need to return to the great Physician as soon as possible. We should not let cancers multiply in our souls. William Plumer (1802–1880) wrote, "He who is determined to see how far he may decline in religion and yet be restored, will lose his soul."[29] As we have seen, backsliding operates like a spiritual cancer: untreated, it can result in dishonor to God's name, personal suffering, apostasy of others, and decay in the church. At best, it is unwise and unloving to take a "wait and see" approach when such consequences are on the line.

The good news is that our Physician is full of wisdom, power, and grace for sinners. He says to us, "I am the LORD that healeth thee" (Exodus 15:26). He is willing to heal us even of the judgments that he himself sent to chasten us (Psalm 39:11, 99:8). "Come, and let us return unto the LORD: for he hath torn, and he will heal us; he hath smitten, and he will bind us up" (Hosea 6:1).

God has grace for his backsliding children. He reveals his wondrous and powerful grace in passages like Hosea 14, the conclusion to Hosea's prophecy about Israel's adulterous backsliding. We will consider here the first three verses of that chapter, which call us to return to the Physician of our souls so that we may find grace:

> O Israel, return unto the LORD thy God; for thou hast fallen by thine iniquity. Take with you words,

and turn to the LORD: say unto him, Take away all
iniquity, and receive us graciously: so will we render
the calves of our lips. Asshur shall not save us; we will
not ride upon horses: neither will we say any more to
the work of our hands, Ye are our gods: for in thee the
fatherless findeth mercy. (Hosea 14:1-3)

Behind all that Israel must "do" in Hosea 14:1–3 is
the action of the Holy Spirit: he initiates and works each
step that any backslider takes toward a cure. Nevertheless,
we see here that every step God's people have taken away
from the narrow way is one more step they must painfully
retrace in their return. While grace absolves the *guilt* of sin,
it does not *cheapen* sin. Rather, grace *aggravates* the pain
of sin, as it must, for it teaches us that the party we have
offended is God—the very God whom we love in Christ
(Westminster Larger Catechism, Question 151).

How, precisely, do we return to the great Physician of
grace that we might be cured of our backsliding? Through
the prophet Hosea, God revealed a threefold way:

- True Repentance
- True Use of the Means of Grace
- True Reaffirmation of Faith

True Repentance

The Lord says to his backslidden people in Hosea 14:1,
"O Israel, return unto the LORD thy God; for thou hast
fallen by thine iniquity." "Return" or "turn back" is a key
word in Hosea for repentance,[30] echoing Moses' forecast

in Deuteronomy of a nation returning to God after suffering discipline in exile.[31] Turning back to God often follows discipline from God, and it is the proper way to respond to such discipline (Revelation 3:19). Only when our departing from God has reduced us to a sense of our poverty do we come to our senses (Luke 15:16–17).

This is no mere change of lifestyle, like going on a low-salt diet or quitting smoking. Such changes can be motivated by sheer selfishness. This is turning from sin back to our covenant God, the breaking of self-will and the rekindling of our love for him. The grammar suggests not just a new orientation or direction towards God, but an actual coming to God. Thomas McComiskey (d. 1996) put it this way: "They are to reenter the sphere of Yahweh's dominion . . . the sphere of Yahweh's love."[32]

Returning to such a Lord is coming home to joy. Richard Sibbes (1577–1635) said that if a man looks to God's creation for salvation and hope, "he is restless still until he come unto Jehovah, who is the all-sufficient, universal good, who fills and fills the soul abundantly."[33] The Lord is our life, and so this act of returning is aptly called "repentance unto life" (Acts 11:18).

What grace it is that the holy God invites, even commands, the backslider to return to him! Fuller wrote, "The Scriptures assure us of the exceeding great and tender mercy of God, and of his willingness to forgive all those who return to him in the name of his Son."[34]

Backslider, he addresses you directly in his compassion: "Return, thou backsliding Israel, saith the LORD; and I will not cause mine anger to fall upon you: for I am merciful, saith the LORD, and I will not keep anger for ever" (Jeremiah 3:12). Behold the love of God in Christ! How he runs to those who come back to him and welcomes them with kisses (Luke 15:20)! How willing he is to come in and have sweet fellowship with those who open the door of repentance (Revelation 3:19–20)!

What does it mean to return to the Lord? What is repentance exactly, especially for the backslidden Christian? The Westminster Shorter Catechism (Question 87) gives us an excellent definition of repentance: "Repentance unto life is a saving grace, whereby a sinner, out of a true sense of his sin, and apprehension of the mercy of God in Christ, doth, with grief and hatred of his sin, turn from it unto God, with full purpose of, and endeavor after new obedience."[35] We see here various steps of repentance—steps that may seem reasonable but that are not necessarily easy to take. For the backslider, as with any sinner battling any sin, true repentance is multilayered, going deep into the heart and mind. Although enabled at every step by the grace of the Holy Spirit, please do not pretend that truly returning from backsliding is a quick or simple process, for it involves at least the following seven components.

1. Recognition of your sinful condition. Repentance and return cannot take place without seeing the grievousness of backsliding for what it is. Notice that Hosea gave a reason for repentance: "for thou hast fallen by thine iniquity." Until we see that we have fallen, and how far, and that this fall was directly caused by our own sin, we will never repent. This is the work of the Spirit who convicts us of sin (John 16:8).

Without the illumination of the Spirit, sinners are blind to their spiritual need. Worse yet, we can become blind to our blindness (John 9:39–41). Backsliding seems particularly susceptible to such blindness, as J. G. Pike (1784–1854) has said: "Secret backsliding is inexpressibly dangerous. Persons who have thus declined from religion may yet maintain its outward forms . . . and feel few or no suspicions respecting their real state."[36] The Lord Jesus rebuked a church in Revelation 3:17 on precisely those grounds: "Because thou sayest, I am rich, and increased with goods, and have need of nothing; and knowest not that thou art wretched, and miserable, and poor, and blind, and naked."

If you get a glimpse of how rotten your heart is, don't resist this illumination. Thank God for it. Remember that the Spirit of conviction is the advance agent of the true Physician. The infected sore must be opened before it can be cleansed. Do not resist him; welcome him and acknowledge the justice of his judgment upon your sin.

2. Remembrance of your past obedience. To the church of Ephesus the Lord said, "Nevertheless I have somewhat against thee, because thou hast left thy first love. *Remember* therefore from whence thou art fallen" (Revelation 2:4–5a, emphasis added). By simply reminding God's people of their past, the Spirit plants deep convictions of spiritual blessings: "Remember the heights from which you have fallen! Remember taking refuge in Christ–how valuable all his benefits were, flowing from his obedience, death, and resurrection! How fervently you desired to be found in him! Remember how sacred the throne of grace was, and how frequently you resorted to it. Remember how close your communion was with God. But where are you now? Remember how far you have fallen from the joyous beginning you made in the way of Christ."

Remembering such things, can the soul respond any differently than Asaph in Psalm 77?

Recalling days when faith was bright,
When songs of gladness filled the night,
I pondered o'er my grievous woes
And searching questioning arose:
Will God cast off and nevermore
His favor to my soul restore? [37]

3. Searching out sin. With repentance, the Spirit grants a holy zeal against sin (2 Corinthians 7:11). He gives you a burning desire to search out any and all sin—known or unknown, original or actual—that impedes your journey to everlasting life (Psalm 139:23–34). Backsliding often results from a lack of regular self-examination, and this must be remedied. Obadiah Sedgwick (1600–1658) said, "The less searching of heart, the less strength of grace always." [38]

You know there cannot be any true, spiritual revival of grace while unrepentant sin remains undiscovered in your heart. Search it out and bring it to light. Face the truth: you are not as you once were! You have lost ground, and the life in your soul has declined. The fruit of the Spirit has withered, the heart has lost its softness, and the throne of grace has lost its sweetness. Search carefully for the real cause of your sad condition. Make constant use of the searchlight of God's Word, as the surest guide in such matters: "Thy word is a lamp unto my feet, and a light unto my path. . . . The entrance of thy words giveth light; it giveth understanding unto the simple" (Psalm 119:105, 130).

4. Grieving over sin. Discovering sin leads to true sorrow for sin, described by the Heidelberg Catechism (Question 89) as "a sincere sorrow of heart that we have provoked God by our sins."[39] An all-consuming sorrow and fiery hatred of sin goes beyond grieving over sin's *consequences;* true grief over sin is concerned with *sin itself*—both original sin in Adam and the disastrous fruits of our actual sins—as an offense to God. So David says of his sin, "Against thee, thee only, have I sinned, and done this evil in thy sight" (Psalm 51:4a).

Paul makes this distinction in 2 Corinthians 7:10, "For godly sorrow worketh repentance to salvation not to be repented of: but the sorrow of the world worketh death." The true sorrow that produces repentance is "godly"—literally "according to God," or God-centered, God-motivated, God-oriented. This kind of grief is rooted in the desire to honor God's name. The sinner learns to grieve over sin more deeply because it dishonors or blasphemes (Romans 2:21—24) the name of the God whom he earnestly desires to love and serve. Have you learned to hate sin because it dishonors God and hinders your enjoyment of him?

5. Confessing your sin. True sorrow must pour out

the backslider's heart before God, owning its own transgressions. "I acknowledge my sin unto thee, and mine iniquity have I not hid. I said, I will confess my transgressions unto the LORD. . . . Lord, all my desire is before thee; and my groaning is not hid from thee" (Psalm 32:5, 38:9).

True confession brings to the Lord the things he himself brought to your attention. The Lord sets the sins of believers in order before them, and they, in return, set their sins in order before God, unreservedly acknowledging the sinfulness of them. And how deeply the Lord delights in such forthright acknowledgment of transgression from his backsliding child: "Only acknowledge thine iniquity, that thou hast transgressed against the LORD thy God. . . . and I will take you one of a city, and two of a family, and I will bring you to Zion" (Jeremiah 3:13–14)!

6. Fleeing from sin. Counterfeit repentance does not yield reformation. It refuses to hate sin wholeheartedly and break from it completely. But godly repentance includes both turning from sin and turning to God. It flees from sin with the heart.

When sin comes like Potiphar's adulterous wife and grasps hold of us, like Joseph we must flee as fast as we can (Genesis 39:12). Is it the love of money? "Flee these things; and follow after righteousness, godliness, faith, love, patience, meekness" (1 Timothy 6:11). Are you enticed by evil desires? "Flee also youthful lusts" (2 Timothy 2:22). Do not play with sin like a toy; cast it away like a deadly rattlesnake. "If ye through the Spirit do mortify the deeds of the body, ye shall live" (Romans 8:13).

True repentance cannot let you continue in sin, so it begs, "Lord, keep me from falling. Let not sin have dominion over me. Fulfill within me, 'whoso confesseth and forsaketh [sins] shall have mercy' (Proverbs 28:13). Grant me grace to flee from sin, to hate 'even the garment spotted by the flesh' (Jude 23), and to 'abstain from even the appearance of evil' (1 Thessalonians 5:22)."

7. Pursuing righteousness. Repentance does not only require "negative" work of confession and fleeing, but also the "positive" work of pursuing God anew. Hebrews 12:12–14 says, "Wherefore lift up the hands which hang down, and the feeble knees; And make straight paths for your feet, lest that which is lame be turned out of the way; but let it rather be healed. Follow peace with all men, and holiness, without which no man shall see the Lord."

Get back on track, fallen runner, and start running after holiness again. At the end of the race stands the Lord himself, ready to embrace you. But the only pathway into his presence is repentance, righteousness, holiness, and obedience to his commands. True repentance produces the fruit of good works (Luke 3:8, Acts 26:20). Do not play games with the Lord. He comes to the tree looking for fruit, or in due time it will be cut down and cast into the fire (Luke 3:9; 13:6–9). Take to heart the words of F. B. Meyer:

> Your life has been dry lately; no tear, no prayer, no fervor. Yet have not met Christ, you have not seen His face for many a long day.... Get quiet and prostrate yourself before God. If people ... want to

detain you with small talk, leave them. Cast yourself down in some solitary place before God, and say, "May God forgive me! May God show me the sin, show me what it is that hinders me, show me what has nearly wrecked my life. Whatever comes, may I not be a castaway, but still be used by Thee through the Holy Ghost for Christ."[40]

Remember, there is no restoration without repentance. Sadly there are many preachers in this land who fit this complaint of Jeremiah all too well: "For from the least of them even unto the greatest of them every one is given to covetousness; and from the prophet even unto the priest every one dealeth falsely. They have healed also the hurt of the daughter of my people slightly, saying, Peace, peace; when there is no peace" (Jeremiah 6:13–14). Don't listen to teachers who offer peace and pardon without brokenness over sin and turning from it. This is not from the Physician of grace. He heals sinners by calling them to repentance (Luke 5:31–32).

How does a backslidden sinner repent? How does the gracious Lord work repentance in us? These questions bring us to the second dimension of returning to the Physician of grace: using the means of grace.

True Use of the Means of Grace

Hosea 14:2 says, "Take with you words, and turn to the LORD: say unto him, Take away all iniquity, and receive us graciously: so will we render the calves of our lips." This verse teaches us *how* to "turn to the LORD"—namely, by using the means of grace which God has provided. It specifically mentions the Bible ("words"), prayer ("say unto him"), and praise ("the calves of our lips"). These are linked together: God's *words* teach us how to *pray* for grace, so that we can offer a sacrifice of *praise*. The most fundamental means of grace is the Word of God.

The means of grace are instrumental to godliness. Psalm 119:9 conveys this succinctly: "Wherewithal shall a young man cleanse his way? by taking heed thereto according to thy word." John Flavel (1628–1691) urged us similarly to guard our hearts by "the diligent and constant use and improvement of all holy means and duties, to preserve the soul from sin, and maintain its sweet and free communion with God."[41] The means of grace are also instrumental in restoring godliness when it decays. So the prophet Hosea instructs the people of God on how to obtain the healing of their backslidings, as promised by the Lord.

But here we must be careful or *the means of grace can become another means of backsliding*. Don't think that using the means can win you merit with God. This is not an effort to balance the record of our evil by doing good. God works through the means of grace to show mercy to hell-deserving sinners. Don't use them as if they were a magic formula which, if performed correctly, will conjure up God's power like a genie from a bottle. God is absolutely free to work when and how he pleases. And don't use the means as a substitute for repentance; God utterly despises the worship offered by hypocrites.

If used rightly the means of grace are a beautiful path

where God meets with us and walks with us, and they are also the tools God uses to rebuild our broken lives. Let us consider some of these means of grace.

The means of the Word of God. "Take with you words," Hosea said. If you would come to God, take with you the very words God provides in the Scriptures. Using the Word of God, the Holy Spirit works faith in the hearts of God's elect. Then, if we fall into sin and therefore compromise that faith, the Word of God restores our faith when we return to the Lord. God's children are not only begotten by the "word of truth" (James 1:18), they are also given "the sincere milk of the word" to drink (1 Peter 2:2). "Thy words were found, and I did eat them; and thy word was unto me the joy and rejoicing of mine heart" (Jeremiah 15:16). When many are falling away, the Word of God binds us to the Savior so that we say, "Lord, to whom shall we go? thou hast the words of eternal life" (John 6:68).

There are several scriptural disciplines that enable us, by the Spirit's grace, to get the rich blessing available in the Word:

- Hearing it preached regularly
- Reading through the Bible day-by-day
- Sharing regular devotions with your family
- Learning a good Scripture-based catechism
- Memorizing particular verses and passages
- Reading Bible-based doctrinal and practical books from solid authors
- Studying the Scriptures yourself on important topics.

But there is one discipline that underlies them all: *meditation* on the Word.

Psalm 1:1–2 tells us that "Blessed is the man" whose "delight is in the law of the LORD; and in his law doth he meditate day and night." To paraphrase Thomas Hooker (1586–1647), meditation is the serious setting of your mind on a truth so as to search it and settle it powerfully in your heart.[42] In meditation your mind hovers over a truth like a bee over a flower to draw out all its sweetness. Like a man standing by a fire in winter, you warm your soul with the energy radiating from the Word. The goal of meditation is to cultivate that inner "life and peace" found in the practice of being spiritually minded (Romans 8:6). Owen explained such spiritual-mindedness as mental activity empowered by grace to engage the heart with truth, so as to produce holy joy and contentment in God.[43]

The Puritans were masters of meditation. Let me sum up their advice: [44]

- Begin with prayer for the Spirit's help (Psalm 119:18).
- Focus on one verse or doctrine—something clear and applicable to your life. It may be a Scripture addressing backsliders (Jeremiah 2; Psalm 25, 32, 51, 130; Hosea 14). Or take a topic like God's character, or Christ's person and work, or the sinfulness of sin.
- Repeat the verse or doctrine to yourself several times, and think about it carefully.
- Preach it to yourself.
- Turn it into prayer and praise.
- Make specific application.

Feed and inflame your soul with the Word. Don't just chew on the Word, but digest it and incorporate it into your life.

The means of prayer. Hosea said, "Take with you words, and turn to the LORD: say unto him, Take away all iniquity, and receive us graciously." Children learn to talk by listening to their parents. Like children, we must learn from the Father the very words that we will speak to him. If someone asks why we must bring particular words to God, Sibbes answers, "It is true; God needs no words, but we do, to stir up our hearts and affections."[45]

So pray the Scriptures back to God:

- If the Bible says, "Thou shalt not," confess the ways in which you *did*. Then run to God and say, "Father, let me never again."
- If the Bible gives a promise to believers, then claim it in prayer by asking God to do what he says.
- If the Bible tells you something about God—and it will tell you much—praise the Lord for who he is, and ask him to let you know him more deeply.

Gurnall wrote, "Prayer is nothing but the promise reversed, or God's Word formed into an argument, and retorted by faith upon God again."[46] So we use Scripture in order to pray truthfully, confidently, and joyfully. This will increase your faith, as Gurnall also wrote:

Furnish thyself with arguments from the promises to enforce thy prayers, and make them prevalent with

God. The promises are the ground of faith, and faith, when strengthened, will make thee fervent, and such fervency ever speeds and returns with victory out of the field of prayer.... The mightier any is in the Word, the more mighty he will be in prayer. [47]

Above all that you ask, pray for the fullness of the Spirit. It is tragic that most prayers focus on physical blessings, especially when most of God's promises focus on spiritual blessings. Pray as Jesus taught us in Luke 11:11–13:

If a son shall ask bread of any of you that is a father, will he give him a stone? or if he ask a fish, will he for a fish give him a serpent? Or if he shall ask an egg, will he offer him a scorpion? If ye then, being evil, know how to give good gifts unto your children: how much more shall your heavenly Father give the Holy Spirit to them that ask him?

The Holy Spirit, experienced through the discipline of prayer, is the daily food we need more than bread and meat.[48]

The means of public worship. When Hosea said that if God would grant us grace, "so will we render the calves of our lips," he meant that the fruition of the Word and prayer in our lives would be public worship, offering praise to God. Calves were the animal sacrifices of the Old Testament's priestly worship, so "the calves of our lips" are the sacrifices of our praises. Hebrews 13:15 tells us we offer such worship through our perfect high priest, Jesus: "By him therefore let us offer the sacrifice of praise to God continually, that is, the fruit of our lips giving thanks to his name."

Of course, it makes a difference with what church you worship. It will hardly cure your backsliding to worship in a backslidden church! But worshipping with a true church—where there is a body of believers worshipping God in the Spirit, rejoicing in Christ Jesus, and putting "no confidence in the flesh" (Philippians 3:3)—can be the means of your rescue from the pit. Envy towards the wicked and mistrust towards God had so darkened Asaph's soul that he almost slipped, but in the sanctuary of God he saw the doom of the wicked and tasted afresh the sweetness of God (Psalm 73).

Find a church that faithfully preaches the Bible and confesses the Reformation doctrines of Scripture alone, Christ alone, grace alone, faith alone, and glory to God alone. Listen to the preaching with a sense of expectation and desire that God would meet with you in the Word. Become a member and pour your life into that church as a living sacrifice to God. Quit complaining and start serving. Cultivate a thankful heart towards your leaders and fellow members. Support the church with your tithes and offerings. Much backsliding could be avoided or remedied simply by faithful participation in a faithful church.

So far we have looked at three means mentioned in Hosea 14:2. But there are others.

The means of afflictions. God uses trials to heal the souls of his backsliding people. God uses sorrow to turn backsliders away from their adulterous love affair with this world so that they seek him again. Hosea 2:6–7 says,

> Therefore, behold, I will hedge up thy way with thorns, and make a wall, that she shall not find her paths. And she shall follow after her lovers, but she shall not overtake them; and she shall seek them, but shall not find them: then shall she say, I will go and return to my first husband; for then was it better with me than now.

In his love God uses suffering to humble us and show us our wicked hearts (Deuteronomy 8:2).

The means of spiritual desertion. Even spiritual desertion serves God's loving purpose. The greatest burden a believer can bear is the sense that God is absent from him, when his prayers meet only silence. The psalmist often describes this kind of loneliness: "How long wilt thou forget me, O LORD? for ever? how long wilt thou hide thy face from me?" (Psalm 13:1). The psalmist's greatest fear is that God would desert him forever, so he begs God not to do that: "Unto thee will I cry, O LORD my rock; be not silent to me: lest, if thou be silent to me, I become like them that go down into the pit" (Psalm 28:1). Thus, the Spirit uses this sense of desertion, or apparent divine withdrawal, as an effective means towards healing because it drives the believer to earnest prayer. Hosea 5:15 says, "I will go and return to my place, till they acknowledge their offence, and seek my face: in their affliction they will seek me early."

We must respond to trials with submission, not resentment and rebellion. We are being disciplined by a loving Father for our good. Hebrews 12:5b–7 says,

> My son, despise not thou the chastening of the Lord, nor faint when thou art rebuked of him: For whom the Lord loveth he chasteneth, and scourgeth every son whom he receiveth. If ye endure chastening, God dealeth with you as with sons; for what son is he whom the father chasteneth not?" If you are suffering under God's hand, then humble yourself and meditate on his character and your sin. Thank him that he did not merely cast you into hell but pursues your heart with relentless love.

Do not, then, resist his pursuit. It is a dreadful thing when God's judgments fall upon a church, yet his people do not turn to him. Jodocus Van Lodenstein (1620–1677) saw it as a proof that God was departing from his church "that our people are persistent and incorrigible in their evil ways (Psalm 55:19), despite the calamities that have brought our nation into such straits."[49] If afflictions come, and our hearts are unmoved, woe to us! Let us cry out all the more for deliverance, beginning by asking for broken hearts.

The means of human accountability. In our individualistic age, we tend to view our spiritual lives as our own concern and no one else's business. But it is not so. God has placed all of us in human society and under human authority. It may be that your backsliding has provoked a censure from your parents, or penalties from the civil government. God commands you to honor authority (Exodus 20:12, Romans 13:1). Do you really expect to rise out of your poor condition if you keep rebelling against God's order?

This is especially important with respect to church discipline. Your elders have a responsibility for your soul, so submit to their admonition and correction (Hebrews 13:17). Your church has a responsibility to correct you privately, to rebuke you publicly, and even to remove you from membership if you do not repent of your public sin (Matthew 18:15–18). The aim of such correction is to restore you from your fall and help you bear your spiritual burdens (Galatians 6:1–2). Love your elders for their efforts to help you. Forgive the imperfections of how they offer that help. Say with David, "Let the righteous smite me; it shall be a kindness: and let him reprove me; it shall be an excellent oil, which shall not break my head" (Psalm 141:5). Christ himself is present in church censures, sovereignly disciplining you (Matthew 18:20, 1 Corinthians 5:4). Submit meekly to their exhortations; let them drive you to Christ. It may very well save your soul on Judgment Day (1 Corinthians 5:5).

One of the best ways to prevent backsliding or arrest it early in its progress is voluntary accountability with a friend (Hebrews 3:13, 10:24–25). An accountability partner is a faithful friend who is willing to ask hard questions on a regular basis and to administer warnings and rebukes when he sees you starting to slip. This is an exercise in true love: "Open rebuke is better than secret love. Faithful are the wounds of a friend; but the kisses of an enemy are deceitful" (Proverbs 27:5–6). If you know that you are prone to backslide in a particular area of temptation, find a faithful friend and build a habit of talking together about how you are doing in that area.

The Word, prayer, public worship, providential affliction, spiritual desertion, and human accountability—the Lord holds all these instruments of healing in his hands. Receive these means of grace and seek God in them. Let them do their good work. Respond to them and exercise yourself in them as a way to lay yourself at the feet of the Lord Jesus in total self-abandonment. The means of grace have no power to help you in and of themselves, but they are the Physician's tools.

This leads us to consider the third aspect of returning to the Physician.

True Reaffirmation of Faith

The final verse we will examine in this chapter, Hosea 14:3, says, "Asshur shall not save us; we will not ride upon horses: neither will we say any more to the work of our hands, Ye are our gods: for in thee the fatherless findeth mercy." Hosea had rebuked Israel for breaking faith with God in many ways, whether it was forging alliances with foreign powers ("Asshur"), or trusting in military might ("horses"), or looking to false gods ("the work of our hands"). Now, if they would return to the Lord, they must renounce all these expedients and alternatives to which they had been resorting and reaffirm their faith in the God of their fathers.

This reaffirmation of faith was not something added

to their repentance; it is the core of returning to the Lord, for the backslider's fundamental problem is one of misplaced trust (Hosea 2:5, 8, 12). "Thou didst trust in thy way, in the multitude of thy mighty men" (Hosea 10:13). Sibbes defined this basic problem as misplaced worship: "What was our fall at first? A turning from the all-sufficient, unchangeable God, to the creature. . . . When we find not contentment and sufficiency in one creature, we run to another."[50] As we cultivate our adulterous love for the world, our knowledge of God grows dim and weak — indeed we reject knowing him (Hosea 4:1, 6; 5:4; 6:6–7). We are willfully and culpably ignorant that he alone is Lord and Savior. So we look to man and man's works to save us.

Perhaps you might object, "But my sin has nothing to do with trusting in the Lord. My backsliding is about sexual lust, or the love of money, or laziness, or stealing at my job, or anger, or rebellion against authority. I'm not even thinking about God when I sin." But as Sibbes pointed out, the root of all sin is a failure to embrace God as our only God.[51] If all the law, and so all our obedience, hangs upon loving God with all our heart (Matthew 22:37–40), so all sin is trusting in idols.[52] Furthermore, not thinking about God *is the problem*. We treat God as irrelevant because we do not really believe that he is the only Lord and Savior. Ray Ortlund writes,

> At issue was the all-sufficiency of Yahweh, with the question perhaps put this way: Where does life, in all its richness and fullness come from? Does it come

from Yahweh alone, or from Yahweh plus others?
If it comes from Yahweh alone, then one will look
obediently to him alone for that life. But if it comes
from Yahweh plus others, then one will spread one's
allegiance around, because Yahweh alone is not
enough.[53]

God's solution is to reunite us to himself in cove-
nantal knowledge (Hosea 2:20). He is and always has been
exclusively the God of his people, as Hosea 13:4 says: "Yet
I am the LORD thy God from the land of Egypt, and thou
shalt know no god but me: for there is no saviour beside
me." Backslidden child of God, the Lord wants you to
know him in a deeper way than you have ever known him
before. He wants you to know him in a way that engages
all of your trust and hope. Do you desire to know him in
this way?

In order to know God in utter dependence, you must
also know yourself. You must know your utter inability
to do any good apart from his grace. You must know the
dire straits in which your backsliding has put you. You
must know the horrible offense of your sins against God.
Bunyan said that sin "is the dare of his justice, the rape of
his mercy, the jeer of his patience, the slight of his power,
and the contempt of his love."[54]

But you must also know the infinite riches of grace
in Jesus Christ. In our spiritual poverty, we have become
orphans, prodigal sons no longer worthy to be called
children of the Father. Sibbes exclaimed, "What is the
church but a company of weak persons?"[55] But Christ

is full of mercy for spiritual orphans: "in thee the fatherless findeth mercy" (Hosea 14:3). His heart beats for the poor and broken in spirit. He delights to give everything to those who have nothing. He was sent for this very purpose, saying, "The Spirit of the Lord GOD is upon me; because the LORD hath anointed me to preach good tidings unto the meek; he hath sent me to bind up the brokenhearted, to proclaim liberty to the captives, and the opening of the prison to them that are bound" (Isaiah 61:1, Luke 4:18). Delight in his kindness toward you!

Charles Wesley (1707–1788), a great poet of the Great Awakening, said it for us all:

> Weary of wandering from my God,
> And now made willing to return
> I hear and bow me to the rod:
> For Thee, not without hope, I mourn;
> I have an Advocate above,
> A Friend before the throne of love.
>
> O Jesus, full of truth and grace,
> More full of grace than I of sin,
> Yet once again I seek Thy face;
> Open Thine arms, and take me in,
> And freely my backslidings heal,
> And love the faithless sinner still.[56]

Dependence means that we build our lives and hopes on a foundation outside of ourselves: the only reliable foundation is our triune God.

The Father. The fountainhead of all restoring grace lies from eternity in the heart of *God the Father*. He loved his elect with an unchangeable and unconditional love while they were yet his enemies. It is his pleasure to give them the kingdom (Luke 12:32).

The Son. The stream of restoring grace flows eternally through *Jesus Christ* who accepted the full cause of the elect and voluntarily took their place to the total satisfaction of divine justice's demands. He agreed to all he would endure at the garden of Gethsemane, the judgment seat of Gabbatha, and the hill of Golgotha to become the sacrifice for them so that they might go free.

The Holy Spirit. All grace comes to us in *the Holy Spirit*. He wisely crafted the Holy Scriptures and speaks today through every word in the Bible. He powerfully formed and supported the holy human nature of Christ in all his trials from womb to tomb. He willingly makes a way for himself into the stony hearts of Adam's children, conquers them, dwells within them despite their remaining sin, and labors to make them holy.

"The Lord is my shepherd; I shall not want. . . . *He* restoreth my soul" (Psalm 23:1, 3). Whether you are a lost sinner coming to Christ for the first time or a backslidden Christian returning to him again or a faithful Christian coming for yet more grace, you can trust in our covenant God. He is utterly faithful, absolutely true, and perfectly good. It is the most freeing thing in the world to be a dependent of the Most High God. Go to him even now and say, "Lord, be merciful unto me: heal my soul; for I have sinned against thee" (Psalm 41:4).

Three
RUNNERS RECEIVING

The Medicines of Grace (Hosea 14:4)

Advances in sports medicine and medical technology have given serious runners a set of advantages few could have imagined even 20 years ago. Through preventive approaches, improved sports equipment, and a more sophisticated understanding of the physiology of exercise and competition, sports medicine helps athletes run smarter, harder, faster, and longer. What it has not done is eliminate injuries.

No matter the level of technology or wisdom or care, everyone who regularly straps on the latest footgear to get back out on the track, the path, or the course will eventually need medical attention. The problem may be a sprained ankle, the pain of "runner's knee," or a dangerous infection spreading from a toe up into the leg. The solution may be rest or something more serious: physical therapy, powerful drugs, or even surgery. Whatever the problem, doctors and bioengineers are on it, working to develop treatments and programs to heal, restore, and strengthen injured athletes.

When the Christian runner receives a spiritual injury and begins to backslide, he must return to the Physician for healing. In the last chapter we looked at the threefold way of returning to our great Physician: repenting, using the means of grace, and depending upon God. Here we focus on the medicine our Physician prescribes and applies to our souls: his own grace. In the deepest sense, God's grace is Christ himself, for he came "full of grace and truth" (John 1:14).

Grace Comes in and through Jesus Christ

No grace is as necessary in divine restoration—or as effective—as a revelation of Christ and his benefits imparted by the Spirit through the Word. The real heartbeat of healing starts when the Holy Spirit reveals our wounded Savior who bled in body and soul with a blood sufficient to "cleanseth us from *all* sin" (1 John 1:7, emphasis added).

When our precious salvation is granted through Christ's blood, and when the Holy Spirit reveals a way of escape in Jesus Christ, there is true, spiritual healing. The soul sees that the obedience of the Lord Jesus opened the way for God's great act of grace. The cross of Christ presents both the most awful exhibition of God's *hatred* of sin as well as the richest manifestation of God's readiness to *pardon* sin. Pardon, full and free, is written in every drop of Calvary's blood, freely offered even to the chief of sinners!

What an unspeakable revelation of grace it is when we see that a way of salvation is available through Christ! This revelation not only reconciles and magnifies all God's attributes, but also serves as a door for the sinful, the vile, and the unworthy. "Christ crucified" shows how God could love such poor, guilty, wandering sinners as we backsliders are. We behold Christ as the answer to all our burdens and wanderings. Oh, the fullness of Christ when revealed by the Spirit! Our weary souls may bring our sorrows and sins to him; in him, we not only get our questions answered, but we also realize that Christ is the answer to them all.

God has made Christ everything to the believer:

- Are we nothing but sin? Christ became sin on behalf of his people to redeem them from it (2 Corinthians 5:21).
- Are we perpetual law-breakers? Christ is the fulfillment of the law (Matthew 5:17, Romans 10:4).
- Are we separated from God? Christ was forsaken by his Father as Judge so that we will never be forsaken by him (Matthew 27:46).
- Are we unrighteous? Christ is the all-righteous one, having merited a perfect robe of righteousness through his active and passive obedience (Isaiah 61:10).
- Are we cursed? Christ died the accursed death as curse-bearer for his elect (Galatians 3:13).
- Are we under Divine wrath? Christ merits, keeps, and applies peace (Isaiah 53:5).
- Are we hell-worthy? Christ descended into hell's pains in his earthly sufferings to prevent hell-bound people from going there forever (Luke 22:44).
- Are we condemned by the truth and righteousness of God? In Christ, "mercy and truth are met

together; righteousness and peace have kissed each other" (Psalm 85:10).

- Are we foolish? Christ is wisdom (Proverbs 8).
- Are we filthy? Christ is "holy, harmless, undefiled, separate from sinners" (Hebrews 7:26).
- Are we prone to temptation? Christ "was in all points tempted like as we are, yet without sin" (Hebrews 4:15).
- Are we spiritually poor? Christ "was rich, yet for your sakes he became poor, that ye through his poverty might become rich" (2 Corinthians 8:9).
- Are we in spiritual bondage? In Christ there is liberty, for "if the Son therefore shall make you free, ye shall be free indeed" (John 8:36).
- Are we weak? Christ is our strength (1 Samuel 15:29, Philippians 4:13).
- Are we prayerless and thankless? Christ is the praying and thanking high priest who sits at the right hand of the Father and never ceases to intercede for his people (Romans 8:34).
- Are we restless? Christ went without rest for thirty-three years, but now he has entered into his rest (Psalm 132:8, Hebrews 1:3), causing his people to rest in him as their prophet, priest, and king who has paid for their entire salvation (Psalm 110).

There is no end to Christ's fullness and beauty. "My beloved is white and ruddy, the chiefest among ten thousand" (Song of Solomon 5:10). When the Holy Spirit reveals his holiness and righteousness, believers experience the truth of Malachi 4:2: "Unto you that fear my name shall the Sun of righteousness arise *with healing* in His wings; and ye shall go forth, and grow up as calves of the stall." Christ's offices and natures form a medicine cabinet out of which the Holy Spirit can remedy every disease that afflicts God's people.

In order to help you to meditate on, receive, and rejoice in the fullness of grace which is in Christ Jesus, this chapter will focus on the three-fold promise of Hosea 14:4, "I will *heal* their backsliding, I will *love* them freely: for mine *anger is turned away* from him." Richard Sibbes wrote about this that we have "the superabounding mercies and marvelous lovingkindnesses of a gracious and loving God to wretched and miserable sinners" opening the door wide for all to come to the throne of grace.[57] And those mercies never end. McComiskey wrote, "The words of Hosea are a treatise on spiritual healing that is as relevant today as it was in his day."[58] So let us open this rich verse and find the spiritual healing of Christ.

It is unspeakably sweet that the Lord comes as a healer, a physician of sick souls. The word "heal" is full of mercy. Charles Spurgeon (1834–1892) preached that it is as though the Lord said, "My poor people, I do remember that they are but dust; they are liable to a thousand temptations through the fall, and they soon go astray; but I will not treat them as though they were rebels, I will look upon them as patients, and they shall look upon me as a physician."[59] Look up to the Lord as your Physician of grace, with hands full of medicine to heal your backsliding.

As we will see, Hosea 14:4 binds our wounds with an unbreakable bandage of three strands: sanctification, adoption, and justification. It is the same three-fold grace that the Westminster Shorter Catechism identifies as the chief benefit of God's effectual or saving call: "They that are effectually called do in this life partake of justification, adoption, and sanctification, and the several benefits which in this life do either accompany or flow from them" (Question 32). Though in the order of our salvation, justification logically precedes the others, Hosea mentions it last because it is the basis for the other two graces.

Perhaps you are thinking, "But how does this apply to the backsliding Christian?" To be sure, those who are already effectually called to salvation do not need a second call when they backslide. Salvation is a single event that need never be repeated. But backsliders do need a renewed experience of these graces in their hearts. That is why returning to the Lord may feel like being converted all over again. Indeed, every Christian needs a daily exercise of faith and repentance as well as daily refreshment in the fundamental graces of his salvation in Christ. And others intent on returning to Christ may discover, as God illuminates their eyes, that they were never truly converted to begin with. Whatever our condition, we may find peace and joy in Jesus Christ.

Sanctifying Grace

So far in Hosea 14, the Spirit-moved prophet has addressed the people and given them words to speak in prayer to God. But in verse 4a, God begins to speak directly to his people: "I will heal their backsliding," How precious is the "I will" of this promise! God is determined to do it, and we know that if he does it, he will do it well. God is able to do whatever he pleases (Psalm 115:3). And it is his good pleasure to "heal their backsliding" — not just the sad consequences of their backsliding but the backsliding itself.

The first medicine of grace is sanctification, that process by which God faithfully and continually works upon our souls, from within and without, to conform us more and more into the image of God's Son, our Savior, Christ Jesus.

God's healing of us through sanctification makes us holy. John Flavel said, "What health is to the heart, that holiness is to the soul."[60] We struggle with our wicked hearts, trying to bend them back toward God, but we discover that our hearts are yet desperately sick and deceitful (Jeremiah 17:9). We then come to God saying, "I cannot!" But he replies, "I will," and follows through by working within us the grace of sanctification.

Note, however, that this promise of healing belongs to the backslidden Christian, not to the hypocrite. Thomas Halyburton (1674–1712) wrote,

> Whereas, all are not the true Israel, who are of Israel; that is who are members of the church by outward profession: it is to be observed, that this promise belongs only to the true Israel; these who are truly engrafted into Christ by true faith. . . . [The promise] is to Israel returning, and seeking a recovery from the Lord.[61]

Only the elect and called of God—those regenerated by the Spirit—can cling to the certainty of God's promise, "I will heal their backsliding." Do not rest on this promise while resting comfortably in sin; rest on this promise of healing while you long for restoration and strive to repent. "Return, ye backsliding children, and I will heal your backslidings. Behold, we come unto thee; for thou art the LORD our God" (Jeremiah 3:22). "I will heal their backsliding" is a promise of victory to the fighter, not security to the sleeper.

Christ will heal the backslidings of those who seek him, believe in him, and love him, so cling to his promise. Spurgeon assured us as to the trustworthiness of that promise:

> The men of Nineveh went to God with nothing to encourage them, but "who can tell?" but the children of God come to him with "shalls" and "wills" to plead. I pray thee, backslider, if thou desirest to return to the Lord this morning, observe the certainty of the text, plead it. God who saith "I will," is not a man that he should lie.[62]

Our need. Sometimes believers do not fully understand that they actually need Christ for everything in the Christian life, despite the clear testimony of Scripture: "But of him are ye in Christ Jesus, who of God is made unto us wisdom, and righteousness, and sanctification, and redemption" (1 Corinthians 1:30). Brakel wrote that backsliding "is sometimes caused by failure to make use of Christ continually unto justification and sanctification," and as a result, sanctification "becomes more a natural work and approximates the virtuousness of unconverted people."[63] Every day must be a gospel day—a day to come to Christ again for more undeserved grace.

Without the union of Christ the Physician with his people, true healing sanctification would never take place, no matter how "religious" we could make ourselves. All sanctification lies in Christ. He said, "Without me ye can do nothing" (John 15:5). Indeed, Walter Marshall (1628–1680) wrote that the only way to get the things you need in order to keep God's law "is to receive them out of the fullness of Christ, by fellowship with him," which, of course, requires that "we must be in Christ, and have Christ himself in us."[64]

The fact that Christ is all our sanctification does not lead to passive quietism. We must not lie back and wait for him to have his way with us—as if such disobedience pleased him. To echo the last chapter, we must exert ourselves to repent and to use the means of grace. We must be the soldiers of the cross whom Isaac Watts described in his hymn:

> Must I be carried to the skies
> On flowery beds of ease,
> While others fought to win the prize,
> And sailed through bloody seas?
>
> Are there no foes for me to face?
> Must I not stem the flood?
> Is this vile world a friend to grace,
> To help me on to God?

Sure I must fight if I would reign;
Increase my courage, Lord.
I'll bear the toil, endure the pain,
Supported by Thy Word.[65]

But to fight and win we must "be strong in the Lord, and in the power of his might" (Ephesians 6:10). We must repent and use the means of grace in dependence upon Christ. We look to him not merely as the provider of our strength but as the one who is our strength. He not only heals but is our health.

The surgery of heaven. Heaven's healing surgery is unique. The same Surgeon who shed his blood to raise his patients from the dead also applies it to heal all their diseases. With Christ as Healer, the healing of sanctification is sure. After all, he died to sanctify his bride: "Christ also loved the church, and gave himself for it; That he might present it to himself a glorious church, not having spot, or wrinkle, or any such thing; but that it should be holy and without blemish" (Ephesians 5:25, 27).

Child of God, have you not experienced Christ as the only Physician able to heal? Has he ever applied the wrong medicine for your spiritual diseases? Has he not also performed all his labors without price, having paid the high cost of your sanctification once and for all with his own precious blood? How well he knows all your symptoms, inclinations, and complaints as his sinful patients!

Yes, sometimes his healing acts are painful, especially when he insists, as a faithful Physician, on probing the depth of the wound. You may have begged him to stop his probing because of the pain; thankfully, he did not and does not stop. He may seem to treat you even more roughly now than before. Only when enlightening grace has shone its light over your past can you see that his roughness was tender love and infinite concern for your eternal welfare (Romans 8:28).

Yet for all the pain caused by the remedy of sanctification, we can trust Christ completely. He is applying medicine to his own body (Ephesians 5:29–30). As believers, we are a part of him, and he is as tender with us as we would be with our own flesh (Ephesians 5:31–32). So if it feels as though we were dying, it is only because he aims to raise us from the dead. We are not in heaven yet; we are being prepared for heaven. Spurgeon said, therefore, that we should expect our current experience to match the current work being done in us: "This is not a palace, but a battle field," so let us walk as "followers of the Crucified."[66]

God will take care of his people. "He brought me up also out of an horrible pit, out of the miry clay, and set my feet upon a rock, and established my goings" (Psalm 40:2). Every believer will learn the paradoxical way of sanctification. United with Christ, they too take up their crosses, deny themselves, and begin to die unto sin. Through his sanctification, they will learn the way of gain through loss.

How glorious are his powerful words, "I will heal their backsliding"! He has sealed them with his own blood. "Who his own self bare our sins in his own body on the tree, that we, being dead to sins, should live unto righteousness; by whose stripes ye were healed. For ye were as sheep going astray; but are now returned unto the Shepherd and

Bishop of your souls" (1 Peter 2:24–25). The surgery our
Lord performs can and will heal us of all our turning away.

Adopting Grace

God's love is from everlasting to everlasting upon his
chosen ones. His love chose them before time began. His
love sent Christ to the cross for their sins. But Hosea 14:4b
refers to a manifestation of the divine love which is a fruit
of the atonement: "I will love them freely, for mine anger is
turned away from him." Samuel Pierce (1746–1829) wrote
that here, God says, "I will love them as freely as if there
had never been sin in them."[67] The love God promises here
is the infinite affection and eternal loyalty that leaps from
his heart when all of his judicial wrath has been satisfied
and nothing is left but love. It is "as if I never had, nor
committed any sin; yea, as if I had fully accomplished all
that obedience which Christ has accomplished for me."[68]

Throughout the Bible, and certainly in Hosea, God's
love for his people is portrayed as both adoptive and conjugal.

It is the conjugal love by which the divine Husband
embraces and kisses his bride on their wedding day. All
the shame of her past is covered by the shining white dress
which he purchased for her by his blood. Hosea was a
living image of this love in his redemption of his unfaithful
wife. Hosea 3:1 says, "Then said the LORD unto me, Go
yet, love a woman beloved of her friend, yet an adulteress,
according to the love of the LORD toward the children of
Israel, who look to other gods, and love flagons of wine."

In Hosea's prophecy, this fruition of love especially
appears in the grace of adoption. Hosea 11:1 says, "When

Israel was a child, then I loved him, and called my son out of Egypt." He was like a father teaching his son to walk, holding up the toddler so that he would not fall (v 3). In verse 4, the Lord declares, "I drew them with cords of a man, with bands of love." His great heart of compassion and unchangeable covenant of grace make it impossible for him to cast his people out (vv 8–9).

It might seem confusing to see God's love described by Hosea both in terms of a man's love for his bride and a father's love for children. Is his love a conjugal love or an adoptive love? These categories jar in our minds. But the revelation of the Trinity answers this question with beautiful clarity. We are the children of the Father and the bride of the Son. When God the Son takes his people as his wife, God the Father looks upon his Son's bride and says, "Welcome, my child, to my family." Our union with Christ guarantees our reception into the household of His Father.

The second medicine of grace by which God heals the backslidden runners in his race is the grace of adoption. In adoption, God takes us into his family to love us "freely," spontaneously, cheerfully, voluntarily, generously, gladly, indulgently, and with nothing in his heart but tender compassions.

Like the father in Christ's parable, he runs to his prodigal child the moment that child returns home, interrupting even our confessions of sin (Psalm 32:5) with showers of hugs, kisses, and calls for a big celebration. Indeed, like the shepherd in another parable, it was he who searched and found you. It is he who heals your backsliding and carries you home on his shoulders, rejoicing.

Sibbes wrote,

> Doth not a father and mother love their child freely?
> What doth the child deserve of the father and mother
> a great while? Nothing. But the mother hath many a
> weary night and foul hand with it. Hath God planted
> an affection in us to love our children freely; and shall
> not God much more, who gives this love and plants it
> in us, be admitted to love freely? [69]

The experience of this adoption fills the soul with joy.
The Spirit of adoption testifies with our spirits that we are
children of God (Romans 8:15–16). God's love becomes
real to us, like water poured into a vessel until it overflows
with hope, joy, and peace (Romans 5:5, 15:13). This is
what the backslidden child of God longs and prays for:
"Restore unto me the joy of thy salvation" (Psalm 51:12).
Spurgeon said, "This is conclusive healing of our backsliding, then we receive beauty for ashes, and the oil of joy for
mourning."[70]

O backslider, may God fill you with the Spirit of
adoption! May he strengthen you with power by his
Spirit in your inner man, so that you are filled to over-
flowing with the knowledge of the love of Christ! Here is
a magnet that will draw and hold firm the most wayward
heart. "Behold, what manner of love the Father hath
bestowed upon us, that we should be called the sons of
God!" (1 John 3:1a). Here we have a mystery to engage
our meditation, food to strengthen our faith, and fuel to
inflame our love.[71]

Justifying Grace

One small word in Hosea 14:4c tells us a great deal: "For mine anger is turned away from him." The word "for" implies that the previous blessings of sanctification and adoption rest upon this mercy.[72] God will heal apostasy (through sanctification) and overflow with affectionate love (as an adoptive father) only when his righteous anger has been turned away because the demands of his righteousness have been satisfied. Indeed, God is a God of righteousness, so the standard of righteousness governs all his relationships. Until the problem of our guilt and offense before him is settled, there can be no peace between us and God.

With respect to Christ's work on the cross, the resolution of our guilt and offense before God is called *propitiation*, turning away God's wrath and satisfying his justice by paying the great price of redemption (Psalm 49:7–8, Romans 3:25–26, 1 John 2:2). When this work that Christ has done is applied to our lives, we are justified.

The third medicine of grace is justification—the act of God's sovereign grace whereby he imputes to the sinner the perfect righteousness of Christ, pardons him of all sin, clears him of all guilt, frees him from all punishment, and gives him a right to eternal life on the sole basis of Christ's perfect obedience and full satisfaction rendered at the cross.

Though our justification in Christ was decreed from eternity (Revelation 13:8), accomplished on the cross (Isaiah 53:11), and proclaimed in Christ's resurrection (Romans 4:24), it is applied to us through faith at the moment of regeneration (Galatians 2:16, Titus 3:5–7) when, in the words of the Westminster Confession of

Faith, "the Holy Spirit doth in due time actually apply Christ unto them."[73]

<u>Distinguishing justification from sanctification.</u> Justification and sanctification possess several common denominators in the believer's salvation:

- Both proceed from free grace and are rooted in the sovereign good pleasures and eternal covenant of triune Jehovah.
- Both are made possible only by and through the head of the eternal covenant, Jesus Christ, acting on behalf of all the elect.
- The elect are the only true subjects of both, and indeed justification and sanctification are inseparable in their application to the soul.
- Both are necessary for salvation, commencing already from the moment of regeneration, although the convicted sinner may not at all view them as secure for him in God through Christ.
- The saints are absolutely helpless to give or take either apart from the grace of God.

Despite these similarities, however, there are important ways in which justification and sanctification differ:

- Justification was accomplished by Christ acting *for* us; sanctification, though rooted in the cross, is actualized by Christ acting *in* us.
- Justification declares the sinner righteous and holy *in* Christ; sanctification makes the sinner righteous and

holy as a fruit flowing *from* Christ.

- Justification takes away the *guilt* of sin (having to do with the legal state of the elect sinner); sanctification takes away the *pollution* of sin (having to do with his daily condition).
- Justification is a *complete and perfect act*, taking place only once; sanctification is an *incomplete process*, progressing daily and not perfected until the God's child is translated to glory.
- Justification gives God's people the *title* for heaven and thus the boldness to enter; sanctification makes them *suitable* for heaven and thus prepares them to enjoy it when that blissful day dawns.
- Justification gives the *right to full salvation* while sanctification provides the *beginnings of salvation*.

Our assurance of justification. Although justification is a legal, objective, instantaneous, complete act, our *assurance* of our justification varies. God may be at peace with us, fully satisfied with his Son's work, but we might not perceive or be assured of that peace. This is one reason why we must daily pray, "Forgive us our debts." The apostle John understood that well and addressed our consciousness of justification with pastoral tenderness:

> But if we walk in the light, as he is in the light, we have fellowship one with another, and the blood of Jesus Christ his Son cleanseth us from all sin. If we say that we have no sin, we deceive ourselves, and the truth is not in us. If we confess our sins, he is faithful and

just to forgive us our sins, and to cleanse us from all unrighteousness. If we say that we have not sinned, we make him a liar, and his word is not in us. My little children, these things write I unto you, that ye sin not. And if any man sin, we have an advocate with the Father, Jesus Christ the righteous: And he is the propitiation for our sins: and not for ours only, but also for the sins of the whole world. (1 John 1:7–2:2)

Christians need daily, sometimes hourly, to confess their sins to God and renew their dependence upon Christ's all-sufficient sacrifice and intercession. We should not sin, but we do sin, so we must wash our consciences in the blood of Christ and count ourselves clean. We must trust, in the words of Samuel Waldegrave (1817–1869), that *"the Lord fully, freely, and at once forgives the backsliding child who turns to Him,* and says, with David, — 'I have sinned.'"[74]

Christians have varying degrees of assurance of their justification when they are converted. Bunyan illustrated this with his allegories of the Christian pilgrimage. The man, Christian, had entered the gate and travelled down the narrow road for some distance before encountering the cross in such a way that his burden of sin fell off his back.[75] But his wife, Christiana, gains a view of the cross and a sense of pardon almost immediately after she enters the gate.[76] Through these figures Bunyan reminds us that a believer may be regenerated and converted (and thus justified) but not gain a subjective assurance of justification until later.

Similarly, when Christians backslide they may lose temporarily their assurance of justification even though those truly born again cannot lose the reality of justification. Peter calls us to grow in our faith, virtue, knowledge, temperance, patience, godliness, kindness, and love, and warns us, "But he that lacketh these things is blind, and cannot see afar off, and hath forgotten that he was purged from his old sins" (2 Peter 1:9).

While David resisted the Spirit's convictions and refused to confess his sins, he suffered a great deal: "thy hand was heavy upon me" (Psalm 32:4). While confessing, he prayed, "Restore unto me the joy of thy salvation" (Psalm 51:12). It was after he confessed that he could celebrate the blessedness of "he whose transgression is forgiven" (Psalm 32:1)—that is, as Paul says, "the blessedness of the man, unto whom God imputeth righteousness without works" (Romans 4:6).

This should motivate us to avoid backsliding. How precious is our sense of peace with God! A good conscience is worth more than all the money in the world. We should guard our conscience by living uprightly, waging war against our inward sins, and living near to God.

But those who have backslidden—this is why you feel such bitterness and deadness in your heart. You have forfeited your assurance of peace with God by cherishing sin. Your works do not save you, but your assurance of justification is connected to your faithfulness. First John 2:2–3 says, "And he is the propitiation for our sins…And hereby we do know that we know him, if we keep his commandments." We *know* that we are joined to Christ in his perfect, sin-atoning work if we walk in obedience to his laws. Persistent disobedience puts a cloud over that sun and leaves us in the shadows.

Therefore it is so sweet to hear God's promise to backsliders: "I will heal their backsliding, I will love them freely: for mine anger is turned away from him."

Hear also the tender words of faithful love that the Lord gave to his bride in Isaiah 54:4–10:

> Fear not; for thou shalt not be ashamed: neither be thou confounded; for thou shalt not be put to shame: for thou shalt forget the shame of thy youth, and shalt not remember the reproach of thy widowhood any more. For thy Maker is thine husband; the LORD of hosts is his name; and thy Redeemer the Holy One of Israel; the God of the whole earth shall he be called.
>
> For the LORD hath called thee as a woman forsaken and grieved in spirit, and a wife of youth, when thou wast refused, saith thy God. For a small moment have I forsaken thee; but with great mercies will I gather thee. In a little wrath I hid my face from thee for a moment; but with everlasting kindness will I have mercy on thee, saith the LORD thy Redeemer. For this is as the waters of Noah unto me: for as I have sworn that the waters of Noah should no more go over the earth; so have I sworn that I would not be wroth with thee, nor rebuke thee. For the mountains shall depart, and the hills be removed; but my kindness shall not depart from thee, neither shall the covenant of my peace be removed, saith the LORD that hath mercy on thee.

Do you wish for a full consciousness of your acquittal so that you can boldly say with full assurance, "I am righteous in Christ, before God, and an heir of eternal life"?[77] Though you may have become like a woman divorced for her adultery, lonely and sad and ashamed, your Husband has the needed grace—in fact, abundant grace—to forgive you completely. Return to your God through repenting, using the means of grace, and reaffirming your faith. Use the medicines Christ provides. He will gather you into his everlasting arms. He will wrap you in his righteousness. He will assure you that his covenant cannot be removed. God delights to comfort his people.

Conclusion

Our Physician has such an abundance of potent medicines to heal his wounded people. In Christ, they are reconciled with God and filled with peace that passes all understanding! Pardon decreed from eternity and purchased in time yields peace and joyful communion. The filthy garments are stripped away. "Behold, I have caused thine iniquity to pass from thee, and I will clothe thee with change of raiment" (Zechariah 3:4). God's people are wrapped in the blessed robe of Christ's perfect, spotless, holy righteousness. Liberty and boldness in the faith becomes their portion; they are free indeed.

They have freedom to leap up and walk with the lame man, praising God in the temple. They confess with Paul, "I know in whom I have believed" (2 Timothy 1:12), and with Job, "I know that my redeemer liveth" (Job 19:25). They can apply to themselves what Christ promises in

Isaiah 61:3 and say, "I have received beauty for ashes, the oil of joy for mourning, the garment of praise for heaviness, that I might be called a tree of righteousness, the planting of the Lord, that he might be glorified." In this act of reconciliation, Christ becomes everything. He is to the reconciled truly the Alpha and Omega (Revelation 1:8), the author and finisher of their faith (Hebrews 12:2), the horn of salvation (Luke 1:69), the Lord of lords (Revelation 17:14), and the Redeemer and Savior (Isaiah 59:20, 1 Timothy 4:10).

Should we not seek such great blessings from the Lord with longing, hunger, and expectant waiting? And when Christ gives us justification, adoption, and sanctification, let us thank him and cherish his grace with all our hearts. We should be zealous to guard the great treasure of grace as our best portion in this life and our only comfort. And when we stumble and backslide, let us go to him again for the medicines of grace.

> Conscience, the Church, the world upbraid:
> Oh, tell me that my sins were laid
> On Him who suffered on the tree,
> And that He groaned and bled for me.
>
> Lord, heal me, and I shall be healed;
> Let pardon to my heart be sealed;
> My wandering, wounded soul restore,
> And let me stray from thee no more.[78]

Four
RUNNERS RECOVERING

The Healing of Grace (Hosea 14:5-9)

When Laura Wilkinson stood atop the diving platform in the final round of her Olympic competition in 2000, she had two strikes against her. First, she was in eighth place behind divers who had performed impeccably. Second, she had broken her foot six months before the Olympic games, severely hindering her training and performance. She was still in pain and had to wear a protective shoe just to climb the diving tower. As she looked down at the water ten meters (32 1/2 feet) below her, she had every reason to be discouraged.

Nevertheless, she said something to herself and did her dive. In fact, she did her dive *excellently*, and Wilkinson walked away from that final round with the gold medal. When asked how it felt to take the gold after facing such obstacles, she replied with the same words she says to herself before every dive, "I can do all things through Christ who strengthens me" (Philippians 4:13).

Christian, it may be that your spiritual life has taken a

fall. Like a runner who has stumbled, you can hardly see the finish line—it looks very far away. Your sin may have broken your heart, dishonored your Lord, and damaged your ability to walk with God. You may have every reason to feel discouraged. But Christ can heal your soul and bring you to the victor's crown. By his grace, you can recover from your fall. It is not only possible for you to survive, but under the healing touch of the Savior you can thrive. When it comes to living for and glorifying the one who died and rose for you, you can do all things through Christ.

We have listened to the Holy Spirit call us, in Hosea 14, to return to the Lord through repentance, the use of the means, and dependence. We have heard him promise his elect people that he has abundant grace for their sanctification, adoption, and justification. Now we will hear his glorious promises to bring his people to full recovery.

Reviving Grace

Israel was not a land of abundant water. It could be a very dry place, especially when the searing hot wind came in off the desert. Lebanon, however, was an exception to the rule. As Douglas Stuart writes, "Lebanon's slopes, moistened almost continually by dew, were places of lush growth year round."[79]

So water in general, and Lebanon in particular, often appears in the Bible as an image of spiritual blessing. This is precisely how Hosea's readers would have interpreted these words:

> I will be as the dew unto Israel: he shall grow as the
> lily, and cast forth his roots as Lebanon. His branches
> shall spread, and his beauty shall be as the olive tree,
> and his smell as Lebanon. They that dwell under his
> shadow shall return; they shall revive as the corn, and
> grow as the vine: the scent thereof shall be as the wine
> of Lebanon. (Hosea 14:5–7)

Again, this was not a promise of agricultural bounty, but a metaphorical promise of spiritual prosperity. The flourishing plants in this image are people, the water is God. The Lord says, "I will be as the dew unto Israel.... they shall revive as the corn." In context, this metaphor refers to the previous "I will" promises of Hosea 14:4: "I will heal their backsliding, I will love them freely: for mine anger is turned away from him." In other words, God will give himself to his people so that they will flourish spiritually under his grace. This is the promised effect of God's three-fold grace: true believers will revive and become increasingly strong, stably rooted, and fragrantly beautiful.

Sibbes wrote, "God's love is a fruitful love. Wheresoever he loves, he makes things lovely."[80] When God comes, he comes like "the dew," refreshing, renewing, invigorating, bringing life, growth, beauty, and fragrance. His gracious presence always changes us. His love makes us lovely. His life makes us lively.

When the Bible speaks of God coming like refreshing water (Isaiah 32:2, 15; 44:1–5; John 7:37–39), it refers to the Third Person of the Trinity, the Holy Spirit. This is the great gift of Jesus to us: "the water that I shall give him shall be in him a well of water springing up into everlasting life" (John 4:14). Christ "baptizes" his people with the Holy Spirit (John 1:33), flooding and drenching them with the Spirit's divine presence and influence.

Halyburton said, "It is not said merely that the Lord will give dew, but that he himself will be as the dew, importing this, that it be a new and near manifestation of the Lord himself, an approach or drawing near of God himself to the soul," which he does "by the fresh supplies of the Spirit of the Lord."[81]

The Filling of the Spirit

To be filled afresh with the Holy Spirit's graces is the great need and secret of all personal healing and spiritual revival. When possessing this fresh infilling in a large degree, God's child possesses every blessing, for it is the pledge of all the rest. Christ instructed his spiritually distraught disciples that his bodily presence was not to be compared with the permanent dwelling of the Spirit among them. Through the graces poured by the Spirit on backsliding believers, they are effectually brought back to God again, and nothing short of this will restore their backsliding souls.

Dear backsliding believer, seek the Spirit's saving graces earnestly and believingly. Seek grace to set out afresh, for God and divine favor, as if you had never walked this path before. Let this be your prayer at the footstool of mercy: "Oh, Lord, revive thy work! Restore unto me the joy of thy salvation! Fulfill thy own Word that 'He shall come down like rain upon the mown grass: as showers that water the earth' (Psalm 72:6)."

Reynolds wrote that God gave us the Hosea 14 image of a prospering and fruitful plant,

> to encourage us in prayer to beg for an answer, not according to the defect and narrowness of our own low conceptions, but according to the fullness of God's own abundant mercies.... God delights to have his people beg great things of him, to implore the performance of "exceeding great and precious promises" (2 Peter 1:4); to pray for a share in "the unsearchable riches of Christ," to know things which pass knowledge, and to "be filled with all the fulness of God" (Ephesians 3:8, 18, 19).[82]

Do you ever beg great things of God? Do you ever dream of what the Holy Spirit might make of you? I am not referring to worldly dreams of power, prestige, pride, and possessions. I am talking about dreams of becoming more like Jesus Christ. He was "like a tree planted by the rivers of water, that bringeth forth his fruit in his season" (Psalm 1:3). His branches were heavy with the fruit of love, joy, peace, patience, kindness, goodness, faithfulness, meekness, and self-control—the fruit of the Spirit who lives in every true believer (Galatians 5:22–24). Why might you not also bear much of this sweet fruit—more than you have ever before?

The Lord Jesus was anointed with "the spirit of wisdom and understanding" (Isaiah 11:2). God gave him remarkable insight even in his human nature to understand and apply the Bible. Why couldn't God illuminate you to see his glory in the Word—so much more that your present light would be like dawn's glimmer compared to the noonday brightness? We are not all teachers, but all Christians have the anointing of the Spirit to teach us (1 John 2:20).

Christ was bold as a lion in the face of angry, violent men. This too is the work of the Spirit whose coming transformed weak Peter into the bold preacher of Pentecost. The Spirit filled others to speak the Word of God with boldness (Acts 4:31). Why not you too?

My point here is not to encourage you to become puffed up but to cultivate holy expectation, and hope in the Lord. Anything we receive of the Spirit is sheer grace and for God's glory, not our own. We are the servants; Jesus is the Lord. But Hosea seems to have wanted to provoke a holy desire in Israel's heart to drink in the dew of the Lord and to grow abundantly. Shouldn't we also have big dreams, big desires, and big prayer requests for our spiritual growth? After all, God is able to do far more abundantly that we can ask or even imagine (Ephesians 3:20). Don't settle for being a spiritual shrimp. Imitate Paul by praying his grand prayers for spiritual growth for yourself, your family, your church, your seminary, and the churches of all nations.[83] For examples of grand prayers of spiritual growth, see Ephesians 1:15–23 and 3:14–21. Cultivate your hope in God's reviving grace.

Sovereign Grace

The essence of backsliding is a descent into the whirlpool of idolatry. But the Lord has never tolerated other gods or worship through images. He regards such practices as hatred against him (Exodus 20:1–6). If we want to flourish, we must do away with idols: "Ephraim shall say, What have I to do any more with idols? I have heard him, and observed him: I am like a green fir tree. From me is thy fruit found" (Hosea 14:8). God's people should have nothing to do with idolatry.

Idolatry denies the sovereignty of God. It cuts the world apart into little domains, each with its own lord who must be appeased. Perhaps it gives a piece of the heavens and earth to God to rule. But in the beginning God *created* the heavens and the earth, and he alone is God. There is no other. He is the God who hears and watches over us all our days. So Hosea reminds us that all this grace he has just described means nothing until we see God as sovereign, the Lord over all in every way.

In a remarkable shift in metaphor in Hosea 14:8, Israel is no longer the flourishing tree but the Lord himself is the tree bearing fruit. It is as if the Lord became Israel, God himself stepping in and fulfilling Israel's responsibility to be fruitful. *That is precisely what happened when God became man.* Israel was supposed to be God's vineyard bearing fruit for righteousness (Isaiah 5:1–7). The very name "Ephraim" means "fruitful" (Genesis 41:52). Fruitfulness stands at the heart of our calling and identity as God's people. But then we discover Jesus Christ announcing that he is the "true vine" and our only hope of bearing fruit is to abide in him as his branches, totally dependent on him for life and support (John 15:1–8). The Lord must do it all. He is the sovereign dew that makes the vine to flourish, and he is the sovereign vine that fills the earth with fruit.

If the heart of backsliding is idolatry, then the heart of returning to the Lord is realizing that Christ is everything for our salvation. Ralph Robinson (1614–1655) wrote, "The Lord Jesus Christ is all things in and to all persons that have a true saving interest in him."[84]

- He is perfect God and he is perfect man.
- He is the Son, and as such, he is our access to the Father and our reception of the Spirit.
- He is the Priest and he is the sacrifice.
- He became our curse and now he is our blessing.
- He is the Prophet and he is the Word.
- He is the King and he is the Servant.
- He is the Mediator and the essence of the covenant.
- He is the Way, the Truth, and the Life.
- He is the Husband who protects and provides and he is the Bread we eat to live.
- He is the Shepherd, the Door of the sheepfold, and the One who laid down his life as the Lamb of God.
- He is our wisdom, righteousness, sanctification, and redemption. We trust in him, love him, and hope in his glorious appearance.
- He is our treasure, exceeding joy, and very great reward.

Christ is all. If you would make any progress in the Christian life, you must embrace him as the sum and substance of your salvation. He says to us still, "From me is thy fruit found."

The Path of Restoration or the Pit of Destruction

Hosea 14:9 concludes the prophet's words with this appeal: "Who is wise, and he shall understand these things? prudent, and he shall know them? for the ways of the LORD are right, and the just shall walk in them: but the transgressors shall fall therein." God offers his wisdom to backsliders. Will we receive it? If we do, then we shall find a path of healing that leads us upward to glory.

God offers us so much. Plumer wrote,

> Here are promised rich supplies of free grace, securing pardon of sin, the indwelling of the Holy Spirit, deep-rooted vigor, increase of grace and of fruitfulness, usefulness to those under his influence, a sweet savor of piety at all times, together with an utter renunciation of idols and self-dependence. [85]

But if we despise God's advice, then we will stumble and fall to our doom. Our backsliding will prove to be apostasy from the faith and we will die in our sins. Either way, God will be vindicated and glorified: "the ways of the LORD are right."

Dear reader, I cannot conclude our consideration of backsliding without asking you whether you are intimately acquainted with backsliding's evils and with the way that God heals this deadly disease. In what condition is your soul? What is your trajectory, the path of restoration or the pit of destruction?

1. *Are you a total stranger of the life of grace?* Then

how poor you are! You have not learned what it means to be converted; you are without the only comfort in life and death, journeying through this life on your own account, without the righteousness of Jesus Christ to satisfy divine justice. If God does not prevent it, you will appear one day before his judgment throne without an intercessor between you and an angry God, Christless and hopeless forever.

Your need is urgent. Fly quickly to God's throne. If you truthfully complain that you lack the ability to fly to God, do not despair; do not leave the Lord alone. Seek grace to confess, "I will not let thee go, except thou bless me" (Genesis 32:26). Follow the advice of Ralph Erskine:

> Do what you can to *fly* up; if you cannot fly, endeavor to *run* without wearying; if you cannot run, endeavor to *walk* without fainting; if you cannot walk because of your broken leg, then will you *creep* to the Physician with it, and hold out the broken leg, the withered arm to him; if you cannot creep, will you *cry* to him; "He hath not said to the seed of Jacob, seek ye me in vain": if you cannot cry, will ye *look* to Him; "Look to me, and be ye saved, all the ends of the earth": if you cannot look to him, will you *long* for him, for "He satisfies the longing soul": *sigh*, and *sob*, and *groan* after him. And if, after all, you think you can do nothing, because of your absolute weakness; then, O will you *wait* on the Lord, and you shall renew your strength; wait on him in the use of means; lie at the pool, and you cannot tell how soon you shall get strength to mount: "Wait, I say, on the Lord."[86]

No case is too hard for the Lord. No sinner, however vile, whose only plea was Jesus' blood, was ever spurned from his presence.

2. *Are you backsliding so far from God that you cannot believe he ever began the good work of saving grace within you?* Filled with your own backslidings (Proverbs 14:14), do you cry out at times, "Oh, to return to the times when gospel sermons were the food of my soul, and secret prayer was kept up with delight! Now a guilty conscience, hard heart, and prayerless life have taken the place of everything I once thought I enjoyed."

If these are the genuine breathings of your soul, let the language of your heart be, "I will wait at the posts of his doors to hear what God the Lord shall say unto me. 'I will look again toward thy holy temple' (Jonah 2:4)." Pray, "turn thou me, and I shall be turned" (Jeremiah 13:18), and to plead his promises: "Is Ephraim my dear son? . . . for since I spake against him, I do earnestly remember him still . . . I will surely have mercy upon him, saith the Lord" (Jeremiah 31:20). Pray, "Lord, if this is thy work within me, confirm it; if not, show me the truth, and begin thy saving work within me." Let these be your petitions.

3. *Are you a backslider who cannot deny having been a subject of God's saving grace, yet you know that you are presently not in the right place before God?* At one time you could answer with Chrysostom when sent a threatening message from the empress, "Go, tell her that I fear nothing but sin"; but now you often lean more toward sin than on grace. If this is you, listen to the advice of Octavius Winslow:

I entreat you, I implore you, I beseech you, to arise and go to your Father, and say unto Him, "Father, I have sinned against heaven and in Thy sight." By all that is tender and forgiving in that Father's heart, — by all that is melting, persuasive, and precious in the work of Jesus, — by his agony and bloody sweat, by his cross and passion, by his death, burial, and resurrection, I beseech you to return! By the honor of that holy religion you have wounded, by all the hopes of glory you have indulged in, by all that is sacred and precious in the memory of the past, and by all that is solemn and real in the prospect of the future, I implore you to return! By the faithful promises of God, by the tender yearnings of Jesus, by the gentle drawings of the Spirit, by all that you will experience in the joy and peace and assurance of a restored soul, by the glory of God, by the honor of Christ, by the nearness of death and the solemnity of the judgment, I entreat, I implore, I beseech you, wanderer, prodigal, to return!

> Return, O wanderer, return!
> And seek an injured Father's face;
> Those warm desires that in thee burn,
> Were kindled by reclaiming grace.
> Return, O wanderer, return!
> Thy Savior bids thy spirit live;
> Go to His bleeding side, and learn
> How *freely* Jesus can forgive.
> Return, O wanderer, return!

Regain thy lost, lamented rest;
Jehovah's melting bowels yearn
To clasp his Ephraim to his breast. [87]

Seek a full return. Avoid the sin of being only slightly affected by your sin so as to be healed incompletely. Beware of escaping your convictions of sin the wrong way; seek probing conviction, true repentance, and total restoration. C. D. Mallary said, "Return, then, with confession and penitence and shame, give up your guilty sins, renounce all dependence upon finite help, and fall into the arms of your injured yet still tender and gracious Savior."[88]

4. *Are you a child of God who can honestly say you are not currently in a condition of "perpetual backsliding" (Jeremiah 8:5), but, rather, in precious restoration (Psalm 23:3)?* Guard revival of soul with a holy jealousy. Remember that you are still in a state of imperfection, snares, and dangers. Despite the healthiness of your present condition, you are not yet beyond the reach of temptation; fresh temptations may lead you to fall into the same sorrowful condition from which you recently emerged, except divine grace interpose to aid you. "As long as I am in the body," wrote Joseph Irons, "I am not yet out of the enemy's gunshot."

This is sanctification: feeling more than ever the strength of sin and the weakness of the flesh, and knowing painfully what it is to be left to yourself, you beg the Lord to keep your soul "as the apple of the eye" (Psalm 17:8), to shine upon it continually with the beams of divine love, and to water it ever more with the divine Spirit and grace. Oh, to ever walk and live to his praise, to know his will and do it, and to be found fruitful "in every good word and work" (2 Thessalonians 2:17)! Being painfully conscious of our own weakness, make the psalmist's request your own: "Hold up my goings in thy paths, that my footsteps slip not" (Psalm 17:5).

Conclusion
A FINAL WORD TO RUNNERS

Wherefore seeing we also are compassed about with so great a cloud of witnesses, let us lay aside every weight, and the sin which doth so easily beset us, and let us run with patience the race that is set before us, looking unto Jesus the author and finisher of our faith; who for the joy that was set before him endured the cross, despising the shame, and is set down at the right hand of the throne of God. (Hebrews 12:1–2)

There is no more noble and rewarding race than that of following Christ. Christian runner, there is no place for self-pity or laziness here. There is glory to be won! Christ has blazed the trail ahead of us; indeed Christ himself is our trail, our living way into God's holy presence. He has overcome, so we too can overcome by his blood. Do not love your life in this world, so that you may gain his glory in the next.

Consider what Christ suffered. He faced the "contradiction of sinners" (Hebrews 12:3). Men argued with him. They accused him of crimes he did not commit. His own disciples opposed his intentions of going to the cross and grieved him by playing ecclesiastical "King of the Hill." Many of his disciples walked away from him when he refused to conform to their worldly expectations. Even those that stayed could not stand with him in his darkest hour. One of his best friends pretended he did not even know him. But Christ persevered.

Christ faced nothing less than the cross and its shame. He let go of all desires for worldly success. He was stripped of all his earthly honor, all his human dignity, even the most basic human rights. They treated Christ worse than we would treat a dog. They beat his body to a bloody pulp, then nailed his tender flesh to a rough cross to hang in agony for hours. Darkness came upon him—not just darkness in the skies but darkness in the soul—such that he cried out, "My God, my God, why hast thou forsaken me?"

But Christ despised the pain and humiliation of the cross for the joy set before him. He counted these agonies a small thing compared to the infinite, eternal happiness of glorifying God through the salvation of sinners. He did not run the race for himself but for us, dear believers! He was bringing many sons to glory.

When we contemplate his agonies of body and soul, we see how very little it takes to make us stumble and turn away from obedience. How often have we sinned for the slightest pleasure, or to avoid the smallest disdain from people? But in the very contrast between our weakness and his strength we find hope. Here is the spiritual champion who can share his victory with us. Runner, when your legs feel like lead and your lungs are burning,

Christ's Spirit can invigorate you again. Look to him, and keep putting one foot in front of the other. When your heart says, "I can't do it; I'm too weak," look at the great cloud of witnesses who have gone ahead of you. They too were weak: Abraham, Moses, David, Peter, and so many others. They too stumbled. But by faith, they ran the race. By faith, they received strength. By faith, and the Spirit's available grace, they got back up when they fell down, and pressed on. By faith, you can do the same.

Christian runner, run the race to the end!

Endnotes

1. William Gurnall, *The Christian in Complete Armour* (Suffolk, 1662–1665; reprint, Edinburgh: Banner of Truth, 2002), 1:2.
2. J. C. Ryle, *The Christian Race and Other Sermons* (London: Hodder and Stoughton, 1900), 156.
3. *The Works of John Bunyan*, ed. George Offor (Glasgow: Blackie and Son, 1854), 3:388.
4. Parts of this book are extensively rewritten from my *Backsliding: Disease and Cure* (Reformation Heritage Books, 1982).
5. Wilhelmus à Brakel, *The Christian's Reasonable Service*, trans. Bartel Elshout, ed. Joel R. Beeke (Reformation Heritage Books, 1995), 4:159–60.
6. Andrew Fuller, *The Backslider: His Nature, Symptoms, and Recovery* (1801; reprint, Solid Ground Christian Books, 2005), 48.
7. Edward Reynolds, "Israel's Prayer in Time of Trouble, with God's Gracious Answer Thereunto: An Explication of the Fourteenth Chapter of Hosea," in Jeremiah Burroughs, et al., *An Exposition of the Prophecy of Hosea* (1865; reprint, Soli Deo Gloria, 1989), 653.
8. See Quartus, "Backsliding," in *Fruitfulness in Christian Service* (Bristol: John Wright and Sons, 1916), 146.
9. Jeremiah 2:19; 3:6, 8, 11, 12, 14, 22; 5:6; 8:5; 14:7; 31:22; 49:4; Hosea 4:16; 11:7; 14:4.

10. Burroughs, et al., *An Exposition of the Prophecy of Hosea* (Reformation Heritage Books, 2006), 488.

11. "The Backslider Characterized," in *The Whole Works of the Rev. Ebenezer Erskine* (Philadelphia: Wm. S. and A. Young, 1836), 1:70. Cf. Henry Melvill, Lectures on Practical Subjects (New York: Stanford & Delisser, 1858), 382–402; The Works of Nathanael Emmons, ed. Jacob Ide (Boston: Congregational Board of Publication, 1862), 5:360–89; The Works of the Reverend and Learned Isaac Watts (London: J. Barfield, 1810), 1:568–74.

12. Plumer, *Vital Godliness: A Treatise on Experimental and Practical Piety* (New York: American Tract Society, 1864), 152.

13. Thomas Vincent, *The Good Work Begun*, ed. Don Kistler (Morgan, PA: Soli Deo Gloria, 1998), 84.

14. Vincent, *The Good Work Begun*, 85–86.

15. Charles H. Spurgeon, *Autobiography* (Cincinnati: Curts & Jennings, 1898), 1:112.

16. Alexander Ross, *The Epistles of James and John, The New International Commentary on the New Testament* (Eerdmans, 1954), 102.

17. Fuller, *The Backslider*, 49.

18. John Angell James, *The Christian Professor Addressed* (New York: D. Appleton & Co., 1838), 300.

19. "Causes and Signs of Declension in Religion," in *The Thoughts of the Evangelical Leaders: Notes of the Eclectic Society, London, During the years 1798–1814*, ed. John H. Pratt (1856; reprint, Edinburgh: Banner of Truth, 1978), 121–22.

20. George Lawson, *Exposition of the Book of Proverbs* (1821; reprint, Grand Rapids: Kregel, 1980), 290–91.

21. *The Works of John Owen* (1850–1853; reprint, Edinburgh: Banner of Truth, 2001), 7:264.

22. Burroughs, et al., *An Exposition of the Prophecy of Hosea*, 348.

23. Plumer, *Vital Godliness*, 157.

24. Erskine, "The Backslider Characterized," in *Works*, 1:68.

25. "Marks of Religions Declension," *Free Presbyterian Magazine* 79, no. 6 (June 1974): 175.

26. Brakel, *The Christian's Reasonable Service*, 4:165.

27. James, *The Christian Professor Addressed*, 307.

28. Fuller, *The Backslider*, 82.

29. William S. Plumer, *Vital Godliness: A Treatise on Experimental*

and *Practical Piety* (1864; reprint, Harrisonburg, VA: Sprinkle Publications, 1993), 148.

30. The root idea of the Hebrew word for "backsliding" is turning. The backslider has turned away, or turned back from following God. So in repentance, he turns once more, turning back in the right direction.

31. Douglas Stuart, *Hosea–Jonah, Word Biblical Commentary* 31 (Nashville: Thomas Nelson Publishers, 1987), 213. See especially Deuteronomy chapters 4 and 30.

32. Thomas McComiskey, "Hosea," in *The Minor Prophets: An Exegetical & Expository Commentary*, ed. Thomas Edward McComiskey (Grand Rapids: Baker, 1992), 1:229.

33. "The Returning Backslider," in *Works of Richard Sibbes*, ed. Alexander B. Grosart (1862–1864; reprint, Edinburgh: Banner of Truth, 2001), 2:253.

34. Fuller, *The Backslider*, 92.

35. The Westminster Confession (Glasgow: Free Presbyterian Publications, 1994), 311.

36. J. G. Pike, *A Guide for Young Disciples* (1831; reprint, Morgan, Pa.: Soli Deo Gloria, 1996), 309.

37. The Psalter (reprint, Reformation Heritage Books, 2003), #210.

38. Obadiah Sedgwick, *Christ's Counsel to His Languishing Church*, ed. Don Kistler (Morgan, PA: Soli Deo Gloria, 1996), 9.

39. Joel R. Beeke, ed., *Doctrinal Standards, Liturgy, and Church Order* (Reformation Heritage Books, 2003), 68.

40. F. B. Meyer, *The Christ-Life for Your Life* (Moody Press, n.d.), 19.

41. *The Whole Works of the Rev. John Flavel* (London: W. Baynes and Son, 1820), 5:423.

42. Thomas Hooker, *The Application of Redemption By the Effectual Work of the Word, and Spirit of Christ, for the Bringing Home of Lost Sinners to God. The Ninth and Tenth Books* (London: Peter Cole, 1657), 210.

43. Owen, Works, 7:270.

44. For a fuller explanation of the art of meditation, see "The Puritan Practice of Meditation," in Joel R. Beeke, *Puritan Reformed Spirituality* (Evangelical Press, 2006), 73–100.

45. Sibbes, *Works*, 2:260.

46. Gurnall, *The Christian in Complete Armour*, 2:88.

47. Gurnall, *The Christian in Complete Armour*, 2:420–21.

48. For additional material on prayer, see James W. Beeke and Joel R. Beeke, *Developing a Healthy Prayer Life: 31 Meditations on Communing with God* (Reformation Heritage Books, 2010); Joel R. Beeke and Brian G. Najapfour, eds., *Taking Hold of God: Reformed and Puritan Perspectives on Prayer* (Grand Rapids: Reformation Heritage Books, 2011).

49. Lodenstein, *A Spiritual Appeal to Christ's Bride*, 87.

50. Sibbes, *Works*, 2:278.

51. Sibbes, *Works*, 2:286.

52. See Matthew 6:24 and Ephesians 5:5 on materialism; see Romans 1:21–26 and 1 Thessalonians 4:5 on sexual immorality.

53. Raymond C. Ortlund, Jr., *Whoredom: God's Unfaithful Wife in Biblical Theology* (Eerdmans, 1996), 49.

54. "Mr. Bunyan's Dying Sayings," in Robert Philip, *The Life, Times, and Characteristics of John Bunyan* (New York: D. Appleton, 1839), 476.

55. Sibbes, *Works*, 2:295.

56. Charles Wesley, "Weary of Wandering from My God," *The Methodist Hymn Book with Tunes* (1904).

57. Sibbes, *Works*, 2:299.

58. McComiskey, "Hosea," in *Minor Prophets*, 1:232.

59. Charles H. Spurgeon, "Backsliding Healed," in *Spurgeon's Expository Encyclopedia* (reprint, Grand Rapids: Baker, 1996), 1:380.

60. *The Whole Works of the Rev. Mr. John Flavel* (London: W. Baynes and Son, 1820), 5:423.

61. Thomas Halyburton, "Divine Influences: or, The Case and Cure of Those under Spiritual Decays," *Halyburton's Works, Volume 1, Faith and Justification* (Aberdeen: James Begg Society, 2000), 1:319.

62. Spurgeon, "Backsliding Healed," 1:382.

63. Brakel, *The Christian's Reasonable Service*, 4:162–63.

64. Walter Marshall, *The Gospel-Mystery of Sanctification* (New York: Southwick and Pelsun, 1811), 52.

65. Isaac Watts, "Am I a Soldier of the Cross?" cyberhymnal.org/htm/a/m/amiasold.htm (accessed September 16, 2011).

66. Spurgeon, "Backsliding Healed," 1:388.

67. Samuel E. Pierce, *An Exposition on the Fourteenth Chapter of the Prophet Hosea* (London: by L. Nichols, 1822), 72.

68. Heidelberg Catechism, Question 60.

69. Sibbes, *Works*, 2:317.

70. Spurgeon, "Backsliding Healed," 1:387.

71. For more on adoption, see Robert A. Peterson, *Adopted by God: From Wayward Sinners to Cherished Children* (Philipsburg, N.J.: P&R Publishing, 2001); Joel R. Beeke, *Heirs with Christ: The Puritans on Adoption* (Reformation Heritage Books, 2008).

72. McComiskey, "Hosea," in *Minor Prophets*, 1:232.

73. Westminster Confession, 11.4.

74. Samuel Waldegrave, "The Backslider Forgiven and Chastised," in *Words of Eternal Life* (London: William Hunt and Co., 1864), 278.

75. John Bunyan, *The Pilgrim's Progress* (1678; facsimile reprint, London: Elliot Stock, 1895), 35–36.

76. John Bunyan, *The Pilgrim's Progress . . . in Two Parts* (London: for W. Johnston, 1757), 2:24.

77. Heidelberg Catechism, Question 59.

78. Joseph Irons, *Grove Chapel Pulpit, Volume 3* (London: Benjamin L. Green, 1851), 204.

79. Stuart, *Hosea-Jonah*, 215.

80. Sibbes, *Works*, 2:330.

81. Halyburton, *Faith and Justification*, 321–22.

82. Reynolds, "An Explication of the Fourteenth Chapter of Hosea," in Burroughs, et al., *Hosea*, 658.

83. A helpful resource here is D. A. Carson, *A Call to Spiritual Reformation: Priorities from Paul and His Prayers* (Baker, 1992).

84. Ralph Robinson, *Christ All and In All* (1868; reprint, Ligonier, Pa.: Soli Deo Gloria, 1992), 2.

85. Plumer, *Vital Godliness*, 171.

86. *The Sermons and Other Practical Works of the Late Reverend and Learned Mr. Ralph Erskine* (Falkirk, Scotland: by Patrick Mair, for John Stewart, Hugh Mitchell, and Peter Muirhead, 1796), 6:221, emphasis added.

87. Octavius Winslow, *Personal Declension and Revival of Religion in the Soul* (New York: Robert Carter, 1847), 233–34. He quotes a hymn titled, "The Backslider," by William Bengo Collyer (1782–1854).

88. Charles D. Mallary, *Soul Prosperity: Its Nature, Its Fruits, and Its Culture* (1860; reprint, Harrisonburgy, Va.: Sprinkle Publications, 1999), 348.

Licensed to Kill
A Field Manual for Mortifying Sin

by Brian G. Hedges

**Your soul is a war zone.
Know your enemy.
Learn to fight.**

"A faithful, smart, Word-centered guide."
– *Wes Ward, Revive Our Hearts*

"Are there things you hate that you end up doing anyway? Have you tried to stop sinning in certain areas of your life, only to face defeat over and over again? If you're ready to get serious about sin patterns in your life—ready to put sin to death instead of trying to manage it—this book outlines the only strategy that works. This is a book I will return to and regularly recommend to others."
Bob Lepine, Co-Host, FamilyLife Today

"Brian Hedges shows the importance of fighting the sin that so easily entangles us and robs us of our freedom, by fleeing to the finished work of Christ every day. Well done!"
Tullian Tchividjian, Coral Ridge Presbyterian Church; author, Jesus + Nothing = Everything

"Rather than aiming at simple moral reformation, *Licensed to Kill* aims at our spiritual transformation. Like any good field manual, this one focuses on the most critical information regarding our enemy, and gives practical instruction concerning the stalking and killing of sin. This is a theologically solid and helpfully illustrated book that holds out the gospel confidence of sin's ultimate demise."
Joe Thorn, pastor and author, Note to Self: The Discipline of Preaching to Yourself

"But God..."
The Two Words at the Heart of the Gospel

by Casey Lute

**Just two words.
Understand their use in Scripture,
and you will never be the same.**

"Rock-solid theology packaged in an engaging and accessible form."
– *Louis Tullo, Sight Regained blog*

"Keying off of nine occurrences of "But God" in the English Bible, Casey Lute ably opens up Scripture in a manner that is instructive, edifying, encouraging, and convicting. This little book would be useful in family or personal reading, or as a gift to a friend. You will enjoy Casey's style, you will have a fresh view of some critical Scripture, and your appreciation for God's mighty grace will be deepened."

Dan Phillips, Pyromaniacs blog, author of The World-Tilting Gospel (forthcoming from Kregel)

"A refreshingly concise, yet comprehensive biblical theology of grace that left this reader more in awe of the grace of God."
Aaron Armstrong, BloggingTheologically.com

""Casey Lute reminds us that nothing is impossible with God, that we must always reckon with God, and that God brings life out of death and joy out of sorrow."
Thomas R. Schreiner, Professor of New Testament Interpretation, The Southern Baptist Theological Seminary

"A mini-theology that will speak to the needs of every reader of this small but powerful book. Read it yourself and you will be blessed. Give it to a friend and you will be a blessing."
William Varner, Prof. of Biblical Studies, The Master's College

---

CruciformPress.com
Ebook downloads $5.45 at http://bit.ly/CPebks

Grieving, Hope and Solace
When a Loved One Dies in Christ
by Albert N. Martin

**There is comfort for the grief.
There are answers to the questions.
The Bible does offer hope, solace,
healing, and confidence.**

**Pastor Albert Martin has been
there.**

"This tender book by a much-loved pastor, written after the death of
his beloved wife, offers comfort to those in tears. A rare guidebook to
teach us how to grieve with godliness, it is relevant to us all – if not for
today, then no doubt for tomorrow."
Maurice Roberts, former editor, Banner of Truth *magazine*

"Albert N. Martin is a seasoned pastor, skilled teacher, and gifted writer
who has given us a priceless treasure in this book. All who read these
pages will, unquestionably, be pointed to Christ and find themselves
greatly helped."
Steve Lawson, *Christ Fellowship Baptist Church, Mobile, AL*

"Like turning the corner and being met by a glorious moonrise, or
discovering a painter or musician who touches us in the deepest
recesses of our being–this little book by Pastor Al Martin has been
such an experience for me. Whether you are a pastor or counselor,
one who is experiencing the pangs of grief, or a member of the
church who wants to be useful to others, you need to read this book."
Joseph Pipa, President, Greenville Presbyterian Theo. Sem.

"Personal tenderness and biblical teaching in a sweet book of comfort. Buy it and give it away, but make sure to get a copy for yourself."
Dr. Joel R. Beeke, President, *Puritan Reformed Theo. Sem.*